MIM

The term mimesis has long been used to refer to the relationship between an image and its 'real' original. However, recent theorists have problematized and extended the concept, allowing new perspectives on such key concerns as the nature of identity. Matthew Potolsky offers a clear introduction to this potentially daunting concept, examining:

- the foundations of mimetic theory in ancient philosophy, from Plato to Aristotle
- three key versions of mimesis: *imitatio* or rhetorical imitation, theatre and theatricality, and artistic realism
- the position of mimesis in modern theories of identity and culture, through theorists such as Freud, Lacan, Girard and Baudrillard
- the possible future of mimetic theory in the concept of 'memes', which connects evolutionary biology and theories of cultural reproduction.

An accessible and broad-ranging study of a term rapidly returning to the forefront of contemporary theory, *Mimesis* will be a welcome guide for readers in such fields as literature, performance and cultural studies.

Matthew Potolsky is Assistant Professor of English at the University of Utah where he teaches literary theory and modern British and comparative literature. He is co-editor of *Perennial Decay: On the Aesthetics and Politics of Decadence* (1999) and has published on theory and late nineteenth-century writing.

THE NEW CRITICAL IDIOM

SERIES EDITOR: JOHN DRAKAKIS, UNIVERSITY OF STIRLING

The New Critical Idiom is an invaluable series of introductory guides to today's critical terminology. Each book:

- provides a handy explanatory guide to the use (and abuse) of the term
- offers an original and distinctive overview by a leading literary and cultural critic
- relates the term to the larger field of cultural representation.

With a strong emphasis on clarity, lively debate and the widest possible breadth of examples, *The New Critical Idiom* is an indispensable approach to key topics in literary studies.

Also available in this series:

Adaptation and Appropriation by Julie Sanders

The Author by Andrew Bennett

Autobiography by Linda Anderson

Class by Gary Day

Colonialism/Postcolonialism – second edition by Ania Loomba

Comedy by Andrew Stott

Crime Fiction by John Scaggs

Culture/Metaculture by Frances Mulhern

Difference by Mark Currie

Discourse by Sara Mills

Drama/Theatre/Performance by Simon Shepherd and Mick Wallis

Dramatic Monologue by Glennis Byron

Ecocriticism by Greg Garrard

Genders by David Glover and Cora Kaplan

Genre by John Frow

Gothic by Fred Botting

Historicism by Paul Hamilton

Humanism by Tony Davies

Ideology by David Hawkes

Interdisciplinarity by Joe Moran

Intertextuality by Graham Allen

Irony by Claire Colebrook

Literature by Peter Widdowson

Magic(al) Realism by Maggie Ann Bowers

Metre, Rhythm and Verse Form by Philip Hobsbaum

Modernism by Peter Childs

Myth by Laurence Coupe

Narrative by Paul Cobley

Parody by Simon Dentith

Pastoral by Terry Gifford

The Postmodern by Simon Malpas

The Sublime by Philip Shaw

Realism by Pam Morris

Romance by Barbara Fuchs

Romanticism by Aidan Day

Science Fiction by Adam Roberts

Sexuality by Joseph Bristow

Stylistics by Richard Bradford

Subjectivity by Donald E. Hall

The Unconscious by Antony Easthope

MIMESIS

Matthew Potolsky

NEW YORK AND LONDON

First published 2006
by Routledge
270 Madison Avenue, New York, NY 10016

Simultaneously published in the UK
by Routledge
2 Park Square, Milton Park, Abingdon, Oxon, OX14 4RN

Routledge is an imprint of the Taylor & Francis Group

Typeset in Adobe Garamond and Scala Sans by
Florence Production Ltd, Stoodleigh, Devon

Library of Congress Cataloging in Publication Data
Potolsky, Matthew.
Mimesis/by Matthew Potolsky
p. cm. – (The new critical idiom)
Includes bibliographical references and index.
1. Mimesis in literature. I. Title. II. Series.
PN56.M536P68 2006
809'.912 – dc22 2005027397

British Library Cataloguing in Publication Data
A catalogue record for this book is available from the British Library

ISBN10: 0-415-70030-2 (pbk)
ISBN13: 978-0-415-70030-6 (pbk)

For Zoe

Contents

Series Editor's Preface ix
Acknowledgements x

Introduction: Approaching Mimesis 1

Part One Foundations 13

1 **Plato's *Republic*** 15
The Invention of the Image 15
Poetry and Censorship: Books Two and Three 17
Mirrors and Forms: Book Ten 21
Poetry and the City 27

2 **Aristotle's *Poetics*** 32
Second Nature 32
Tragedy, Plot and Reason 38
The Tragic Effect 43

Part Two Three Versions of Mimesis 47

3 ***Imitatio*: Rhetorical Imitation** 49
Mimesis as a Cultural Practice 49
Roman Echoes 54
Ancients and Moderns 59
Genius, Originality and the Anxiety of Influence 65

4 **Theatre and Theatricality** 71
Spectacle and Spectator 71
Theatrum Mundi 75
Acting, Naturally 81
'The Never Ending Show' 87

5 Realism **92**
The Grapes of Zeuxis 92
Reflection and Convention 97
Realism and Sincerity 102
Pygmalion's Folly: Anti-Realism 107

PART THREE MIMESIS IN MODERN THEORY **113**

6 Mimesis and Identity **115**
Psychic Mimesis 115
Identification: Freud 118
The Mirror Stage: Lacan 125
Performing Race and Gender 128

7 Mimesis and Culture **136**
Sympathetic Magic 136
Mimicry and the Mimetic Faculty 140
Mimetic Desire: Girard 145
Simulacra and Hyperreality 150

Conclusion: Memetics **157**

GLOSSARY 163
SUGGESTIONS FOR FURTHER READING 165
BIBLIOGRAPHY 168
INDEX 173

Series Editor's Preface

The New Critical Idiom is a series of introductory books which seeks to extend the lexicon of literary terms, in order to address the radical changes which have taken place in the study of literature during the last decades of the twentieth century. The aim is to provide clear, well-illustrated accounts of the full range of terminology currently in use, and to evolve histories of its changing use.

The current state of the discipline of literary studies is one where there is considerable debate concerning basic questions of terminology. This involves, among other things, the boundaries which distinguish the literary from the non-literary; the position of literature within the larger sphere of culture; the relationship between literatures of different cultures; and questions concerning the relation of literary to other cultural forms within the context of interdisciplinary studies.

It is clear that the field of literary criticism and theory is a dynamic and heterogeneous one. The present need is for individual volumes on terms which combine clarity of exposition with an adventurousness of perspective and a breadth of application. Each volume will contain as part of its apparatus some indication of the direction in which the definition of particular terms is likely to move, as well as expanding the disciplinary boundaries within which some of these terms have been traditionally contained. This will involve some re-situation of terms within the larger field of cultural representation, and will introduce examples from the area of film and the modern media in addition to examples from a variety of literary texts.

Acknowledgements

I would like to thank Stacey Margolis, Howard Horwitz, Barry Weller, John Drakakis, Liz Thompson and Megan Becker-Leckrone, who all offered valuable comments on this book. I also owe a debt of gratitude to the students in various incarnations of my course on mimesis, who helped me to work out many of the formulations and approaches to the topic that inform this book. Work on this book was supported in part by a Faculty Fellowship from the University Research Committee at the University of Utah, to whom I am grateful.

This book is dedicated to my inimitable daughter Zoe.

INTRODUCTION
Approaching Mimesis

Mimesis is among the oldest terms in literary and artistic theory, and it is certainly among the most fundamental. It so defines our way of thinking about art, literature and representation more generally that we rely on the concept even if we have never heard of it or do not know its history. Most often (but inadequately) translated from the Greek as 'imitation', mimesis describes the relationship between artistic images and reality: art is a copy of the real. But this definition hardly accounts for the scope and significance of the idea. Mimesis describes things, such as artworks, as well as actions, such as imitating another person. Mimesis can be said to imitate a dizzying array of originals: nature, truth, beauty, mannerisms, actions, situations, examples, ideas. The word has been used to describe the imitative relationship between art and life, as well as the relationship between a master and a disciple, an artwork and its audience, and the material world and a rational order of ideas. Mimesis takes on different guises in different historical contexts, masquerading under a variety of related terms and translations: emulation, mimicry, dissimulation, doubling, theatricality, realism, identification, correspondence, depiction, verisimilitude, resemblance. No one translation, and no one interpretation, is sufficient to encompass its complexity and the tradition of commentary it has inspired. Nor can any one translation account for the range of attitudes mimesis evokes. Mimesis is always double, at once good and bad, natural and unnatural, necessary and dispensable. It is the sincerest form of flattery as well as the trade of pirates and plagiarists, the signal behaviour of great artists as well as apes, parrots and children.

The many meanings, attitudes and metaphors that mimesis elicits demonstrate its overriding significance to Western thought. Mimesis has been a recurrent, even obsessive, concern for artists and philosophers for thousands of years. There are few major discussions of art that do not engage the concept at least obliquely. Not all art is, strictly speaking, mimetic, but the very concept of art, for Western culture at least, is inconceivable without the theory of mimesis. For the ancient Greek philosopher Plato, who introduced the term into literary theory over two thousand years ago in his dialogue the *Republic*, art 'merely' imitates something real. It is an illusion, he argues, and thus needs to be distinguished from truth and nature. It is no exaggeration to say that the entire history of literary theory has turned upon challenges to, and modifications or defences of, this definition. As the twentieth-century French philosopher Jacques Derrida has written, 'the whole history of the interpretation of the arts of letters has moved and been transformed within the diverse logical possibilities opened up by the concept of *mimesis*' (1981: 187). Without a knowledge of mimesis, one simply cannot understand Western theories of artistic representation – or even realize that they are theories rather than facts of nature.

But mimesis has always been more than a theory of art and images. From its very origins in Greek thought, mimesis connected ideas about artistic representation to more general claims about human social behaviour, and to the ways in which we know and interact with others and with our environment. More recently, it has informed research in psychology, anthropology, educational theory, feminism, post-colonial studies, political theory, and even neo-Darwinian biological speculation, as well as literary and artistic theory. The word mimesis originally referred to the physical act of miming or mimicking something. Plato and his student Aristotle carried this common human behaviour over to the realm of artistic production: art imitates the world much as people imitate each other. The ability to create and be moved by works of art, they suggest, is an essential part of what it means to be human. Their argument underlies many familiar ideas about art and representation. Take, for example, the claim that great art conveys universal truths. We commonly believe that art, unlike laws, rituals or social structures, is not limited in its value or significance to a particular age or culture, and that it speaks to a transcendent human nature. Or take the equally familiar idea that representations have irresistible effects on human behaviour. Although we know that books, movies and video games are not 'real', we nevertheless believe that they have a profound influence on young viewers and readers in particular. Contemporary psychologists call this the 'Werther effect', after a novella by the German writer Johann Wolfgang von Goethe, *The Sorrows of Young Werther* (1774), which is said to have led many readers to imitate the suicide of its tragic young hero. Recent experiments, however, have demonstrated that children are much better able to imitate live actions than those they see on television (see Hayne *et al.*, 2003). Adults also tend to imitate children as much as children imitate adults. These facts should be obvious, yet the ancient Greek idea that mimesis strikes at and speaks to something deep within human nature continues to shape our everyday beliefs about and practical relationships to art and literature.

The impossibility of disentangling the aesthetic, social and psychological meanings of mimesis is a recurrent crux in the history of literary and artistic theory. As the classics scholar Stephen Halliwell has noted, Western thought has historically been divided between two fundamental ideas about art that come from the combined approaches of Plato and Aristotle. The first idea imagines that art reflects the world as it is, that it copies a material reality outside the work. The second idea defines art as a self-contained 'heterocosm' that simulates a familiar world, and in effect copies our ways of knowing and understanding things (Halliwell, 2002: 5). These ideas entail significantly different assumptions about the relationship between art and human nature, in particular, about whether mimesis has its roots in nature and objective reality or in culture and custom. According to the first idea, mimesis gives a more or less accurate rendering of what is, and thus depends for its production and reception on the reality of the material world and the unchanging operations of the human eye or ear. So long as we can perceive the world as it really is, we should be able to discern whether a work accurately imitates reality. According to the second idea, however, mimesis need not reproduce what actually is, only give a persuasive, or 'lifelike', simulation of it. Because the effectiveness of this simulation depends in large part upon our particular beliefs about and ways of knowing the world, it is inextricably bound up with mind and culture. If the first idea is true, art is like a mirror turned to the world. If the second idea is true, it is like a mirror implicitly turned to the spectator and his or her beliefs. In neither case, however, can we think about mimesis without some reference to human psychology or culture.

As we shall find, the first idea about mimesis is often asserted but is very difficult to demonstrate, particularly for literary works, which cannot literally 'mirror' anything. The most interesting debates in the history of mimesis concern the second idea. For Aristotle, who first proposed this idea, mimesis is effective if it resonates with basic cognitive operations. Art appeals to reason, specifically to our inherent sense of what is probable or necessary, and thus should be comprehensible across cultures and historical periods. But recent theorists have pushed Aristotle's suggestion that art simulates the world much further, arguing that mimetic artworks appeal only to our conventional beliefs about reality. The word convention describes a customary and usually (but not necessarily) unspoken rule or agreement that guides social life or artistic production. Conventions are collective beliefs that over time or by force of habit gain the status of objective facts. It is conventional, for instance, for students to raise their hands if they want to ask or answer a question in class, much as it is conventional for a sonnet to concern love, and for landscape paintings to exclude prominent human figures. There is nothing inevitable about these conventions, but at the same time we never think to question them. They comprise a kind of 'second nature' within culture.

According to conventionalist accounts of mimesis, artist and audience share a set of conventions so familiar that neither side recognizes that it is trafficking in conventions rather describing objective reality. The mimetic effects of the artwork are produced by a proper 'match' between the work and the expectations of its audience. Fidelity to convention, not fidelity to nature, is the source of mimesis. The conventionalist account makes mimesis radically dependent on the social and historical context in which a work is produced and received. Different cultures have different ways of describing reality, and different historical periods are dominated by different conventions, so a work that 'matches' the expectations of one culture or historical period might seem strange or artificial for another. Conventionalist accounts of mimesis are common in debates about the nature of artistic realism, the subject of chapter 5, but I shall also stress the extent to which other forms of mimesis also rely for their effect on a combination of social and artistic conventions. For example, mimesis in the theatre, the subject of chapter 4, depends just as much on the conventional expectation that audience members sit silently and treat the stage as if it were a separate world as it does on the actor's ability to feign a character. If the audience members insisted on conversing with the actor or walking up on stage during the performance, then the theatrical illusion would be difficult to sustain. We shall also find, however, that some of the most powerful recent discussions of mimesis, informed by psychology, anthropology and evolutionary biology, explain conventions as only one aspect of a more primal mimetic drive in human beings that transcends cultural and historical differences. Seen from this perspective, following a convention is just another form of imitation.

Despite its centrality to the history of theory, or perhaps because of it, the word mimesis has led a rather uneventful intellectual life. It is, of course, a key term for literary and artistic theory. But simply tracing out the various uses of the word itself over the history of criticism would not be especially illuminating. The theory of mimesis remains so tied to its origins in the works of Plato and Aristotle that few thinkers before the twentieth century sought to redefine or rethink it in any substantial way. The term is monolithic, an overarching concept that theorists are compelled to accept or reject, but do not feel free to decisively transform. An article on mimesis from the *Dictionary of the History of Ideas* summarizes the eighteenth-century attitude toward the topic in these terms: 'The idea of imitation having been thoroughly discussed and analysed, nothing much was left to be done' (Tatarkiewicz, 1973–4: 3, 229). A similar sense of belatedness and inevitability marks the entire history of mimesis, despite the fact that much was, and has continued to be, done with the idea.

This does not mean, however, that mimesis lacks a significant history, or that it has not taken distinct forms in different cultural contexts. True to its definition, mimesis is an excellent mime, changing its name and interpretive scope to suit each new environment. For this reason, I will treat mimesis not as a single coherent theory organized around a clearly defined key term, but as what the German scholars Gunter Gebauer and Christoph Wulf call a 'thematic complex' (1995: 309). The theory of mimesis comprises a constellation of philosophical problems, familiar images and metaphors, conceptual oppositions and archetypal human relationships that are bound together by the influential writings and cultural authority of Plato and Aristotle. My aim in this book is to catalogue the elements of this thematic complex, trace out their interrelations and define their uses at key historical moments. The theory of mimesis develops out of a series of returns to the Greek context. The concept shifts and changes with each return and in each of the philosophical and cultural contexts in which it arises. This history is itself mimetic, based on changing relationships between the 'original' and its myriad 'copies', between the Greek masters and their devoted or rebellious disciples. At no point, however, does it go wholly beyond the framework Plato and Aristotle established, despite repeated claims to the contrary by theorists.

The mimetic quality of the history of mimesis poses a conceptual problem. Since all historical writing relies on mimetic techniques such as narration, example and illustration, a history of mimesis risks becoming hopelessly entangled in the story it tells. 'The fact that mimesis cannot be represented without the use of mimetic processes', Gebauer and Wulf comment, 'poses the fundamental problem of theory formation in reference to our object. What is the relation between the representational and the represented world?' (1995: 21). With this question in mind, I have combined various approaches to the thematic complex of mimesis that together will provide a concise 'portrait' of the subject. Like the theory it follows, the book unfolds through a series of returns to the writings of Plato and Aristotle. Rather than telling a single linear narrative, I have presented several overlapping but relatively autonomous historical narratives, each structured by one of four key themes common in discussions of mimesis since antiquity: the imitation of role models; theatre and theatricality; the idea of realism; and the foundation of mimesis in human behaviour. My discussion of these themes centres on different historical periods, but they are not unique to any one period. In constructing this highly intricate history, I have looked to works spanning nearly twenty-five centuries and drawn from many disciplines: art theory, literature, philosophy, theatre history, psychology, sociology and anthropology. My ultimate aim is less to define mimesis itself than to document the many and often conflicting ways in which artists and philosophers from Plato to the present have tried to define it.

The book opens with two chapters on the origins of the theory of mimesis in the writings of Plato and Aristotle. Beginning with a discussion of the word's etymology and early usage, these chapters reconstruct the definition of mimesis in Plato's *Republic* (chapter 1) and in Aristotle's *Poetics* (chapter 2), and describe the cultural and political contexts in which the concept develops. Both philosophers distinguish mimesis from reality, but they take very different approaches to its nature and effects. Whereas Plato regards mimesis as a dangerous and potentially corrupting imitation of reality, Aristotle treats it as a foundational aspect of human nature, with its own internal rules and proper effects. And whereas Plato associates mimesis with violence, extreme emotions and the irrational, Aristotle regards it as a rational and fully valid practice. These two positions define the contours of the debate over mimesis in Western culture, and continue to inform discussions over the value of art.

The next three chapters of the book turn to an exposition of three major thematic elements that have shaped discussions of mimesis, and the social and artistic conventions commonly associated with them. Chapter 3 looks at the role of rhetorical imitation, that is, the imitation of exemplars and role models, in ancient Roman and Renaissance thought. Beginning with the eighteenth-century English poet Alexander Pope's suggestion that imitating Homer is no different from imitating nature, the chapter considers how this notion of mimesis, in the guise of the Latin word *imitatio*, comes to supplement the Greek focus on art as an imitation of nature with theories about the way artists should imitate one another. *Imitatio* defines mimesis in terms of tradition, convention and example. The chapter traces this interpretation of mimesis from its origins in Plato and Aristotle to its centrality for ancient Roman writers such as Horace, Seneca, Virgil and Longinus, and then to Renaissance figures in fifteenth- and sixteenth-century

Europe, such as Petrarch, Erasmus and Sir Philip Sidney, who self-consciously imitated the Romans. The chapter concludes with an account of the decline of *imitatio*, and the origins of our current notions of originality, in early Romantic thought at the end of the eighteenth century. For the Romantics, *imitatio* is merely conventional, and cannot be the activity of true genius.

Chapter 4 focuses on another thematic version of mimesis: theatre and the theatrical. Where *imitatio* frames mimesis as a relationship between the poet and his or her role models, theatre foregrounds the relationship between art and its audience. Theatre greatly complicates traditional models of mimesis based on the examples of art and poetry, since it is grounded on the relationship between spectacle and spectator, and not on any single material 'quality' of theatrical artwork itself. Theatre is a way of seeing and acting, governed by social and artistic conventions, and not a singular thing. The chapter begins by tracing the origins of this idea of theatre from the early Latin church father Saint Augustine, who wrote in the fourth century CE, to current theorists of theatre and performance such as Richard Schechner and Josette Féral. I then turn to the development of the so-called *theatrum mundi* metaphor, which imagines the world itself as a kind of theatre. This section focuses on a reading of Shakespeare's *Hamlet*, a veritable compendium of attitudes toward theatrical mimesis. The chapter then discusses modern ideas about actors, acting and the theatricality of social and political life, moving from the eighteenth-century French philosophers Jean-Jacques Rousseau and Denis Diderot to twentieth-century theorists such as the German playwright Bertolt Brecht and the American sociologist Erving Goffman.

Chapter 5 looks at debates over the nature of literary and pictorial realism and, more broadly, at the way mimesis defines the relationship between art and the world. What makes a work of art seem real to us, and why is realism so often considered the ideal for artistic representation? The chapter addresses these questions by returning to the two historical poles for understanding mimesis I introduced above: art as a mirror and art as a simulation. I trace these contrasting attitudes towards realism from ancient Greece to the development of linear perspective in fifteenth-century painting, and then to the rise of nineteenth-century novelistic realism and its two most important twentieth-century critics,

Erich Auerbach and Georg Lukács. The final section of the chapter looks at some varieties of anti-realism. Critics of realism, from the late nineteenth-century writer Oscar Wilde to the twentieth-century French critic Roland Barthes, suggest that art impoverishes itself, or deceives its audience, if it seeks only to depict the world or reflect the prevailing conventions of its age.

The last two chapters of the book focus on twentieth-century theories of mimesis and, in particular, on recent accounts of the relationship between mimesis and human nature. For many twentieth-century figures, mimesis is a primary human activity, not a secondary and derivative repetition of something else. These figures seek to extend the theory of mimesis beyond art and representation to questions of identity, desire and language. While they often critique Plato, the theories in fact revive the ancient association of mimesis and human behaviour that motivated Plato and Aristotle. Chapter 6 considers the importance of imitation to the origins and development of identity. The chapter begins with the work of the late nineteenth-century sociologist Gabriel Tarde, who saw all social behaviour as forms of imitation, and then looks at the notion of 'identification' in the thought of the influential twentieth-century psychoanalysts Sigmund Freud and Jacques Lacan, as well as among contemporary theorists of race and gender who both draw upon and greatly complicate this notion. Identification, for Freud, is a form of unconscious imitation, in which we model ourselves upon another person. Lacan and other theorists point to the ways in which Freud's theory highlights the social origins of individual identity. They argue that 'natural' gendered behaviours or racial differences are not expressions of an inner essence but effects of imitated conventions.

The final chapter considers the role of mimesis in twentieth-century theories of culture. The chapter begins with a brief discussion of mimetic themes in the writings of Rousseau, and the nineteenth-century German social theorist Karl Marx. Both Rousseau and Marx suggest that society is governed by forms of mimesis, although they disagree over whether the imitation is conscious or unwitting. I then turn to late nineteenth-century anthropology, which commonly drew upon the traditional language of mimesis to explain pre-modern ideas about magic and the nature of images. For intellectuals of the next generation, this theory of 'sympathetic magic' offered new ways of thinking about mimesis in modern society as well. I look first at a group of theories from the 1930s and 1940s, proposed by Walter Benjamin, Roger Caillois and Theodor Adorno, that cast mimesis as a foundational human tendency and a distinct way of knowing the world. The chapter then turns to the French literary critic René Girard's theory of mimetic desire, first developed in the 1960s, which suggests that all of our wants are driven by imitation of others and not by inherent needs. The chapter concludes with an account of the concept of the simulacrum developed by French theorists of the 1960s and 1970s. The simulacrum, a copy without a single original, stretches the Platonic understanding of mimesis to its limits, and offers a new means of analysing the 'magical' effects of modern media culture.

My conclusion moves from the psychological and anthropological account of mimesis in the last two chapters of the book to a brief discussion of the recently developed field of 'memetics'. Drawing upon genetics and evolutionary biology, memetics tries to understand the spread of ideas according to the model of Darwinian evolution. Just as sexual reproduction spreads genes, so acts of imitation spread what theorists call memes. This theory is only in its infancy, but it has become a controversial topic and constitutes the latest addition to the thematic complex of mimesis.

Given the concise nature of this book, and the great complexity of the theory I discuss, my account of mimesis might usefully be seen as a series of snapshots (the metaphor is inevitably mimetic) that will cumulatively provide readers with a framework, a family album as it were, for understanding mimesis. There are many other potential snapshots that one might take from the long history of the concept. Readers might go on to explore the crucial role mimesis plays in Christian thought, for example, or the ways in which post-colonial theorists have illuminated the refashioning of Western ideas about mimesis by peoples subjected to Western imperialism. The concept of imitation is also important to film theory and to the Marxist concept of ideology, and it arises as well in a wide variety of scientific fields, from experimental psychology to cognitive science, and even robotics. The list of suggested readings at the end of this book offers some additional ways into the thematic complex of mimesis. This complex, as we shall find, is remarkably rich. In fact, the theory of mimesis might be said to have the paradoxical status of the map in the 1935 fable by the Argentinian writer Jorge Luis Borges, 'On Exactitude in Science' (1998). This map is so detailed that it exactly covers the territory it surveys, and soon becomes all but indistinguishable from it. The theory of mimesis has so woven itself into the texture of Western thinking about representation that the first step in understanding the concept is recognizing that it is a concept, a map, as it were, of the relationship between art and nature, and not a perennial feature of the landscape.

PART ONE

Foundations

1

PLATO'S *REPUBLIC*

THE INVENTION OF THE IMAGE

The ancient Greek philosopher Plato provided the first and unquestionably the most influential account of mimesis. Although he refers to mimesis at many points in his career, the most important discussion of the topic comes in his dialogue the *Republic*, a wide-ranging work of political, ethical and literary theory that was probably written around 380 BCE. Plato does not simply comment upon an existing notion of mimesis in this dialogue but radically redefines art as essentially mimetic, as a representation of something else. This notion is so fundamental to the way we understand art that it is no exaggeration to claim that art itself, as a distinct human product, is a Platonic invention. Plato's theory of mimesis is very complicated, but is made even more so by the fact that, in this dialogue as elsewhere in his works, Plato speaks through the figure of his deceased teacher Socrates, so we are never certain whether any given utterance should be taken seriously or ironically. Nevertheless, the effect of this theory is so profound that no discussion of art and representation can avoid some engagement with Plato's definition. To this extent, the history of literary and artistic theory begins with Plato's account of mimesis.

The word mimesis can be traced to the fifth century BCE, but it is rare before Plato adopted it in the following century, and its specific meanings remain the subject of scholarly dispute. Mimesis derives from the root *mimos*, a noun designating both a person who imitates (compare the English word 'mime') and a specific genre of performance based on the imitation of stereotypical character traits. Very little is known about these performances. In the *Poetics*, Aristotle mentions 'the mimes of Sophron and Xenarchus' as a form of 'imitation by means of language alone' (1951: 9). Other scattered references occur in Greek writing, but there are no surviving examples of these performances. Some scholars have claimed they were religious rituals, but it is now generally accepted that Aristotle refers to a Sicilian dramatic genre in which actors would depict scenes from the lives of commoners (Else, 1958: 76). While it is difficult to discern a clear development in meaning, early uses of mimesis and related words refer chiefly to the physical mimicry of living beings by bodily gesture or voice, and only more rarely to paintings or statues. Yet even in its earliest uses, mimesis never simply meant imitation. From the very beginning it described many forms of similarity or equivalence, from visual resemblance to behavioural emulation and the metaphysical correspondence between real and ideal worlds (Halliwell, 2002: 15).

As the French classical scholar Jean-Pierre Vernant has argued, Plato's use of the word mimesis marks a crucial turning point in the history of Greek ideas about art: the emergence of a recognizably modern notion of the image (*eidolon*). Prior to Plato, Vernant notes, Greek culture regarded images as an actualization or 'presentification' of what they represent. Archaic statues of gods, for example, were understood not simply as illusionistic depictions of a deity but as an actual revelation of a divinity that would otherwise be invisible (Vernant, 1991: 153–5). Plato transforms mimesis into a far-reaching technical concept that defines the representational arts as such. It is, Vernant suggests, 'the first general theory of imitation' in any Western culture (1991: 180). This theory is hardly neutral in its aim or effect, for Plato's innovation fundamentally devalues the image. Where archaic Greek thought regarded images as embodiments, Plato classes the image with a group of behaviours and phenomena that had previously been understood as distinct. Miming, emulation, pictures, mirrors, shadows, echoes, dreams, reflections and even footprints are henceforth regarded as 'semblances'. They are grouped together in their difference from, but resemblance to, real objects (Vernant, 1991: 166). The effect of this transformation is radical, redefining art as mere appearance, not a real thing. Neither craft nor creation, it is now an image or imitation of something else. Plato's definition at once makes and unmakes art, defining it as a recognizable category of human action, and yet draining it of any independent reality.

POETRY AND CENSORSHIP: BOOKS TWO AND THREE

Plato approaches mimesis in two contexts in the *Republic*: first in books two and three, and then in book ten. In neither context does Plato explicitly set out to define the arts. Rather, the question of mimesis emerges from the discussion of broader topics: political organization, education, the ideal of justice and the nature of philosophical knowledge. But mimesis is never simply an aesthetic category. Instead, it is posed as a potential threat to the ideals of justice and reason. In a turn of argument that will inform almost every theory we will encounter in this book, Plato ties mimesis to much broader questions of human nature and political life. These associations arise from the argumentative context in which Plato introduces his theory. Towards the beginning of the dialogue, Plato's speaker Socrates proposes constructing a city as a way of more effectively discerning the constitution of the human soul. Much as a just city should be governed by its wisest citizens (the philosophers), so the just soul should be governed by its best part (reason). This city will allow Socrates to argue for the ideal of reason on a larger canvas than the individual life. Mimesis will be introduced in the course of this discussion of the city, and so becomes a microcosm for the problems of political and ethical theory that Socrates takes up.

Socrates begins by imagining a city in which each individual performs one task in accordance with his or her nature, and for the good of the collective. There is a farmer, a weaver, a carpenter, and so forth. Each focuses on his or her proper task and does not try to do anything else. Even when this first city expands to encompass trade and wage labour, what scholars have termed Socrates' 'principle of specialization' remains intact. But Socrates' auditors believe that the citizens of this city could not do without certain pleasures and would soon come to reject the frugal life Socrates proposes. So in place of his 'healthy' city Socrates begins to describe what he calls a 'feverish city' (Plato, 1991: 49). It is here that the word mimesis makes its debut in the dialogue. This unhealthy city, Socrates suggests, will need luxuries along with its basic functions. Chief among these luxuries is mimesis:

> Then the city must be made bigger again. This healthy one isn't adequate any more, but must already be gorged with a bulky mass of things, which are not in cities because of necessity – all the hunters and imitators, many concerned with figures and colors, many with music; and the poets and their helpers, rhapsodes, actors, choral dancers, contractors and craftsmen of all sorts of equipment, for feminine adornment as well as other things.
>
> (Plato, 1991: 50)

This list associates art and mimesis with superfluity, effeminacy, violence, theatricality and social hierarchy. Arriving along with hunters, workers, actors and the makers of women's adornments, mimesis is defined as secondary and unhealthy. It is a luxury, not a necessity. Even before he formally introduces his definition of art, then, Plato separates mimesis from the real, the rational and the essential, and equates it with pleasure and emotion rather than truth, reason and the necessities of life.

The first discussion of artistic mimesis as such comes somewhat later in book two. Having set out the basic structure of his city, Socrates considers those who will defend its citizens, the guardians. Here again, the account of mimesis arises from a discussion of politics and conduct. Socrates and his auditors worry that those individuals best suited to protect the city from external threats might themselves threaten the populace, since the aggression they properly turn outward can also be turned inward and threaten the city itself. For this reason, Socrates outlines a course of education for the guardians. It is often said that Plato simply opposes poetry, but Socrates in fact advocates the use of stories in education. Noting that young children are easily moulded and readily assimilate themselves to 'the model whose stamp anyone wishes to give' them, he argues that the guardians can be shaped ethically by the stories they hear (Plato, 1991: 54). Socrates imagines this shaping quite literally.

He compares it to the way gymnastics shapes the body, and suggests that mothers and nurses can shape the souls of children with tales in much the same way that they shape their bodies by massaging them as infants. While gymnastics and massage give the child a beautiful form, stories give them a beautiful soul. Later in the dialogue, Socrates describes this beauty as a kind of ethical 'grace'. The properly trained guardian will act intuitively in the interest of justice, just as a wrestler's body moves intuitively in the midst of a match.

Stories are central to this training, but they must be used carefully. Inaugurating a line of argument that we still encounter in discussions of the influence of television and movie violence on young viewers, Socrates claims that artistic imitation inevitably begets behavioural imitation. Telling stories to young children will produce imitations of the good or bad actions that the story represents. Socrates makes this point explicitly in book three: 'Or haven't you observed that imitations, if they are practiced continually from youth onwards, become established as habits and nature, in body and sounds and in thought?' (Plato, 1991: 74). The initial 'stamp', whether good or bad, repeats itself in the conduct of the child throughout life. For this reason, Socrates suggests, 'we must supervise the makers of tales' to ensure that the guardians are stamped with the right behaviours. The rulers of the city will have to 'persuade nurses and mothers' to tell the young only 'the approved tales' (Plato, 1991: 55).

Socrates wants to control both the subject of the tales, and the way (and by whom) they are told. The guardians, he claims, should be prevented from hearing 'untrue' stories about the gods. As Philippe Lacoue-Labarthe has noted, every story Socrates would censor describes acts of 'depropriation': violence, adultery, political usurpation, shape-changing, trickery, madness (1998: 130). The first story he excludes from the education of the guardians concerns strife within the divine family: the epic poet Hesiod's tale of how Uranus tried to prevent the birth of his son Chronos, who in revenge castrated his father (Plato, 1991: 55). Above all, Socrates notes:

> it mustn't be said that gods make war on gods, and plot against them, and have battles with them . . . provided that those who are going to

> guard the city for us must consider it most shameful to be easily angry with one another.
>
> (Plato, 1991: 56)

In book three, Socrates continues his list of prohibited stories and behaviours. To encourage manliness and bravery among the guardians, Socrates forbids stories about the torments of the underworld, any depictions of heroes lamenting their fate, laughing uncontrollably, disobeying their superiors or being immoderate in their desires for sex, food or money. Following the principle that imitation begets imitation, he wants to prevent the guardians from repeating any activities that would be unbecoming of the defenders of a city. Even though Socrates gives stories an important place in the education of the young, then, he follows his initial implication that mimesis is excessive, unnatural and false. Indeed, mimesis is an effective educator precisely because it is false. Its power to circumvent reason turns ethical training into a matter of automatic and unthinking imitation rather than rational choice. It acts like a drug, Socrates suggests, that is useful when administered correctly, but dangerous when given indiscriminately (Plato, 1991: 60).

Socrates extends his account of the ethical influence of mimesis on its audience to the effects of literary style on the performer. Like their content, the form of stories shapes the souls of those exposed to it. This is true both of children and adults, as Socrates subtly broadens his account of mimesis from the training of the young to a generalized psychology of artistic response. Socrates divides narration into three types: simple, mimetic and mixed. In simple narration, the poet speaks in his or her own voice, telling a story without taking on the role of any of the characters. This is the style of historical narrative. In mimetic narration, by contrast, the narrator imitates the character in voice or gesture, as in a theatrical performance: 'he gives a speech as though he were someone else' (Plato, 1991: 71). Mixed narration, the main style of epic, and, as many commentators have noted, of Platonic dialogue, combines the two methods. At times the poet narrates, and at times he or she mimics the voice of a character. It is important to note that ancient Greek poetry was spoken, usually by travelling performers called rhapsodes, who would recite or act out scenes from Homeric epics and other works. Literate individuals would read poetry out loud even when alone. So when Socrates defines the different types of narration, he has in mind a performance rather than a strictly written literary style. He pictures the rhapsode or the reader 'becoming' the character he or she speaks about.

This context explains what might otherwise seem to be an odd claim. Socrates suggests that the guardians should not be mimetic narrators, and that what they imitate in any context should be severely limited. He gives four reasons for prohibiting such imitations, each of which draws a connection between mimesis and human behaviour. First, the mimetic narrator, for Socrates, is inherently a liar. He conceals his personality behind that of his character, and thus opens up the possibility of other deceptions. Second, mimetic narration violates the principle of specialization. The only task of the guardians is to protect the city, but imitating others is akin to performing their tasks as well: 'he'll hardly pursue any of the noteworthy activities while at the same time imitating many things. . . . The same men aren't capable of doing both.' Third, the imitator cannot avoid a certain contamination by the object of imitation. The guardians must be careful to mime only appropriate behaviour, 'so that they won't get a taste for the being from its imitation' (Plato, 1991: 73–4). For this reason, Socrates insists that they should only imitate good and courageous men, rather than women, slaves, bad men, inhuman sounds (thunder, animals) or the insane. This leads to the fourth reason Socrates prohibits most imitation among the guardians: the character of the imitated inevitably reflects upon the imitator. A good man, Socrates notes, will feel ashamed at imitating a common man: 'he can't stand forming himself according to, and fitting himself into, the models of worse men'. Indiscriminate imitation fragments the personality, makes one 'double' or 'manifold' (Plato, 1991: 75–6). In the end, Socrates argues that the mimetic poets should be exiled from the republic.

MIRRORS AND FORMS: BOOK TEN

The aims of this exile become further reaching when Socrates returns to his discussion of mimesis in book ten of the *Republic*. We have seen how the discussion in books two and three subtly moves from the effects of mimesis on children to its potential effects on adults. Book ten redefines these effects in philosophical terms. Socrates returns to the status of mimesis after he has finished outlining the structure of his republic and the human soul. His reflection on the soul has persuaded him, he says, that he was entirely correct in banishing the mimetic poets. The best republic and the best life are both governed by reason, but mimesis is contrary to reason in almost every way. Socrates' inquiry into the opposition between mimesis and reason is complicated and takes up much of book ten. For the sake of simplicity, we can distinguish three grounds upon which Socrates bases his critique: the reality of mimesis; the relationship of mimesis to knowledge; and the effects of mimesis on the emotions.

Plato begins his discussion of art in book ten by challenging the reality of mimesis, its status as a thing with unique properties. This challenge follows upon a distinction Socrates introduced in a famous allegory he constructs in book seven. The so-called 'allegory of the cave' imagines humans as prisoners watching shadows cast on the wall of a cave. What these prisoners take to be reality is, from the perspective of philosophy, mere illusion. Since they, and implicitly we, know nothing beyond the shadows they see, the prisoners can have no grasp of reality, nor any sense of why the world as they know it is false and incomplete. All they know from birth to death are shadows, not realities. Socrates imagines one prisoner being released from his chains and turning towards the light and the actual objects that cast the shadows, and then working his way out of the cave to look directly at the sun. This prisoner's new perspective is akin to philosophical education. What common people take to be reality is for the philosopher less real than truths grasped by means of reason alone. As the German philosopher Martin Heidegger suggests, in his essay 'Plato's Doctrine of Truth' (1947), the allegory of the cave begins a revolution in the Western concept of truth. No longer a fundamental trait of the material world, truth now resides in the intellect alone (Heidegger 1998: 181–2). In Plato's rendering, the world itself becomes an imitation, and is thus always suspect.

This redefinition of truth has important consequences for the account of mimesis in book ten. Artistic images, Socrates suggests, are only shadows of the things they imitate, which present the physical appearances of things, not their rational truth. Images are, to this extent, inherently corrupting for the philosopher, regardless of whether they depict virtue or vice. Socrates advances this argument with two analogies. The first analogy compares mimesis to a mirror. Socrates asks his auditors to imagine a great craftsman, who has the ability to create everything in heaven and earth. The auditors doubt the existence of such a craftsman, but Socrates notes that his power is in fact quite simple. 'It's not hard' to make all things, he claims:

> if you are willing to take a mirror and carry it around everywhere; quickly you will make the sun and the things in the heaven; quickly the earth; and quickly yourself and the other animals and implements and plants and everything else that was just now mentioned.
>
> (Plato, 1991: 279)

This metaphor mocks the idea that art requires special skills and methods. The craftsman does not in fact make anything, but only passively reflects what already exists, and does so 'quickly', almost automatically. Mimesis produces mere 'phantoms', not real things. It is at once dependent and deluded, just as a mirror is empty and inessential without something to reflect. The same thing, Socrates argues, is true of artistic images, which reflect the world but have no essence of their own. 'The painter is also one of those craftsmen, isn't he?' Socrates asks. Yet the mirror-bearing 'craftsman' foolishly believes that he does in fact create something. Not content simply to produce couches and tables, the artist wants to usurp the power of the gods, and claims to create the heavens and the earth, and even seems to 'create' himself. But this power is an illusion, for the artist does not make the 'being' he represents, he only reflects 'something that is like the being, but is not being' (Plato, 1991: 279).

To reinforce this association of art and 'mere' appearance, Socrates introduces another analogy, based on his so-called theory of forms. He asks his auditors to imagine three kinds of couches. The first couch is 'in nature'. This is the idea of a couch produced by a god (Plato, 1991: 279). The second couch is material, the kind made by a craftsman. The third couch is an imitation painted by an artist. Socrates argues that each couch has a different relationship to reality and truth. The real maker of any couch is the god. The one true couch is the rational idea of a couch, and hence the 'original' for any other couch. Platonic philosophy uses reason to identify the singular essence of the good or the beautiful – its unitary 'form'. Along the same lines, Socrates argues, the god's couch is most real because it is purely conceptual. Although it is material, and thus real in the colloquial sense, the craftsman's couch is nevertheless at a remove from the true reality. The craftsman looks towards the rational form of a couch when he makes any given material couch. He crafts an approximation of the original, gives material form to the concept in his work. The imitated couch, in turn, is twice removed from the real one. The painter relies entirely upon the craftsman's couch when he or she makes an imitation. Ignorant of the god's couch, the painter gives us only the appearance of a material couch. Moreover, the painter can only represent one side of the object. He or she imitates how the couch looks from one limited perspective, not what it essentially is. 'Therefore', Socrates concludes, 'imitation is surely far from the truth . . . because it lays hold of a certain small part of each thing, and that part is itself only a phantom' (Plato, 1991: 281). The artist may be able to fool children and madmen, but those in possession of reason will see through the ruse.

Socrates next turns to the threat that mimesis poses to knowledge. The ability of the imitator to craft any object, he notes, has long deceived people. Imitators may appear to know about the objects and actions they depict, but this knowledge is illusory. Socrates points to the example of the great epic poet Homer, whose works the *Iliad* and the *Odyssey* had a standing in Plato's culture akin to the standing of the Bible for much of European and American history. Socrates complains that Homer often depicts battles and civic deliberation, but could not have had any real knowledge of warfare or governance. Indeed, by his very nature, the imitator lacks knowledge: 'Do you suppose', Socrates asks:

> that if a man were able to make both, the thing to be imitated and the phantom, he would permit himself to be serious about the crafting of phantoms and set this at the head of his own life as the best thing he has?
>
> (Plato, 1991: 282)

Mimesis is not serious; it is mere play rather than true knowledge. Artists such as Homer 'don't lay hold of the truth' but only mime the appearance of wisdom (Plato, 1991: 283). Socrates introduces another tripartite distinction to press his point. The user of any object, he argues, will have the most intimate knowledge of its virtue, beauty or utility. Only a flute player, for example, can adequately judge the quality of a flute. The user, like the philosopher, looks towards the rational idea of an object, considers the object against the concept that defines it, and the purpose it serves. The flute maker, by contrast, needs the user's guidance to ensure that the product he or she crafts will perform as it should. While the user has genuine knowledge about flutes, the maker can only hold what Socrates defines as good or bad opinions about them. Imitators have neither knowledge nor opinion about what they imitate. A painted flute cannot be played and teaches us nothing about what a flute really is or does. Imitation is twice removed from genuine knowledge, just as it is from reality. This analogy again tries to strip mimesis of any pretension to craft. All three figures might well be considered craftspeople: the user makes music, the maker makes a flute, and the imitator makes a painting. But for Socrates, imitators merely mirror the work of others, and have no knowledge of what they represent.

As a source of knowledge, Socrates continues, imitation is not only dishonest but also potentially corrupting, and appeals to the worst part of the psyche. Like an optical illusion, it introduces confusion into the soul, and undermines the powers of reason and calculation. Socrates uses the image of a stick placed into a pool of water to explain this effect: although this stick is really straight, it looks bent in water. The eyes alone might be fooled by appearances and lead one to conclude that the water has bent the stick. Only rational knowledge of how water affects the appearance of objects reveals the truth. Whereas the senses give us contradictory evidence, reason and calculation lead to truth. The imitators actively appeal to the confusion of the senses. They elevate shadows over truth: 'imitation keeps company with the part in us that is far from prudence' (Plato, 1991: 286). The representational arts, to this extent, are inherently opposed to reason and philosophy, and forever dwell at the bottom of the cave.

Having challenged the reality and rationality of mimesis, Socrates turns to the effects of art on our emotions. His main target now is tragedy rather than painting. This shift deserves some attention. Although he defines all of the representational arts as mimetic, Socrates had clearly been concerned from the start with stories. In books two and three he focuses on the effects of myths and methods of narration; throughout book ten he takes aim at Homer, and he begins this book by arguing that the city should exclude all poetry, not just the imitative kind. But the first two steps in the argument about mimesis in book ten are based on an analogy with painting and mirrors rather than stories or poems. The movement from visual to linguistic imitation is problematic. Language does not imitate in the same ways that images do. As even ancient philosophers recognized, words are signs with conventional meanings, not images of what they name. The word 'mirror' does not reflect in the same way that a physical mirror does. Socrates tries to bridge this gap between words and images with an argumentative sleight of hand: he suggests that his criticisms of imitation based on sight also apply to imitation based on hearing. Accordingly, he treats poetry as yet another form of illusion. But language, of course, entails more than hearing, much as painting entails more than mere seeing. By reducing poetry to perception, Socrates can extend his claim that mimesis requires no skill and has no reality to tragic drama.

The analogy between art and optical illusions, as we saw, suggests that mimesis divides the mind, setting the claims of the senses against reason. Something similar occurs in the context of tragedy. All poetry, Socrates argues, imitates 'human beings performing forced or voluntary actions', reflecting upon the consequences of those actions and feeling pain or pleasure in response (Plato, 1991: 287). The division between action and emotion in tragedy is similar to the division between the senses and reason in the visual example. Tragedy imitates human actions as a means of stirring our emotions, and thus divides us against ourselves. Socrates elucidates this point with the example of a man who has lost a son. Although this man would be grieved by his loss, reason instructs him not to express his emotion in public. He is divided between his emotions and his intellect, between what Socrates characterizes as a childish and irrational desire to indulge in his pain and a mature recognition that he must stoically accept what fate has brought him. Tragedy, however, encourages us to indulge in suffering. It is easier to imitate violent emotion than rational contemplation. Emotion is noisy and visible, while the prudent individual is difficult to understand from without. Much as the painter imitates what a couch looks like rather than what it is, so tragedy only shows what human character looks like from the outside. Thus it is drawn to, and inherently appeals to, the emotional part of our nature, producing 'a bad regime in the soul of each private man' (Plato, 1991: 289).

Since it appeals to the emotions rather than to reason, tragedy has far-reaching consequences for the audience. Just as children imitate the stories they hear, audiences at the theatre identify closely with what they see depicted on stage. Even the best among us are led to 'give ourselves over to following the imitation', and suffering along with the hero (Plato, 1991: 289). Mimesis produces sympathetic imitations in the viewer, the effects of which go beyond the space of the theatre. Tragedy teaches us to enjoy the expression of emotion in other contexts as well, and thus weakens the hold reason has over our souls. Having enjoyed the emotional displays on stage, we become less ashamed of expressing emotions in our own lives: 'the pitying part [of the soul], fed on these examples, is not easily held down in one's own sufferings' (Plato, 1991: 290). Rather than being ruled by reason, we are now ruled by emotion. This danger is, for Socrates, cause enough to extend his earlier exile of the mimetic poets from the republic. Following Homer and the tragedians only brings misery: 'And if you admit the sweetened muse in lyrics or epics, pleasure and pain will jointly be kings in your city instead of law and that argument which in each instance is best in the opinion of the community' (Plato, 1991: 290). No longer satisfied to exile only the mimetic poets, Socrates now banishes all poetry from his republic.

POETRY AND THE CITY

Why would Plato's most extensive and influential discussion of mimesis come in the midst of a dialogue on political and ethical theory? This question has long been a matter of debate among scholars, and it is clear from his arguments throughout the work that Plato wants his readers to reflect on the relationship between mimesis and politics. It is no accident that Socrates responds to the danger of mimesis with political acts: official censorship and exile. And throughout the dialogue, Plato insistently joins the seemingly insignificant act of mimicry to the very fate of the community. Both discussions of mimesis in the *Republic* begin by defining and criticizing artistic mimesis, but end with considerations about the safety of the republic and the 'regime' of the soul. Indeed, the word mimesis covers a striking range of human activity for Plato. Initially, and most obviously, it describes the activity of the representational artist. Both poetry and painting imitate the real: material objects in painting, and human action and emotion in poetry. But mimesis is also a part of education. Children imitate the stories they hear, and this imitation shapes their souls. Thus Socrates insists on supervising the tellers of tales and ensuring that their narratives do not engender problematic imitations in the audience. Socrates also associates mimesis with artistic performance. Rhapsodes and actors imitate, and thereby take on the qualities of, the characters they describe. In order to prevent mimetic contamination, Socrates argues that the rulers of the republic must supervise the kinds of imitations the guardians perform, as well as those they hear. By the end of book ten, mimesis has come to characterize the whole of aesthetic response. No longer a quality of just the pupil or the performer, mimesis describes the identification of an audience with the spectacle on stage. Swept up by tragic emotion, the members of the audience imitate privately the sufferings they see on the stage. From creation to reception, art and influence are defined by mimesis.

This progression from individual artist to collective response, and from the behaviour of children to the nature of the soul, makes artistic mimesis a microcosm of political life. It encompasses both the individual and the social world, and affects citizens from birth to adulthood. Plato offers hints throughout the dialogue that his subject is larger than stories and pictures. Mimesis enters the dialogue along with luxury and political corruption, and the initial discussion of poetry concerns the education of the guardians needed to protect the city from its enemies and from itself. The stories Socrates chooses to exclude from his educational programme nearly all describe strife within the community. Throughout the dialogue, moreover, Plato subtly opposes mimesis to the ideals of masculinity. He associates imitation with women, children and the insane, all of whom were expressly excluded from Athenian political life. His specific prohibitions, and even his seemingly incidental examples, often highlight the association of mimesis with those excluded from political participation. The actors, for example, arrive in the city along with the makers of women's adornment, and it is nurses and mothers whose storytelling must be controlled. The guardians are forbidden to imitate slaves, and Socrates worries that painters might trick 'children and foolish human beings' into believing they are true craftsmen (Plato, 1991: 281). Tragedy, finally, encourages men to cry like women and children.

Two of Plato's parables in the *Republic* also hint at the political implications of mimesis. The most obvious is the allegory of the cave, which a number of twentieth-century philosophers have linked to modern political methods. The cave depicts political life as a kind of totalitarian theatre, in which unknown and unseen individuals present the chained prisoners with images that distract them from the truth of their condition. What seems real to the people is in fact a show intended to keep them pacified. The political implications of the cave are by no means coincidental, for the prisoner who is freed and leaves the cave is a figure for Plato's ideal philosopher king. Having seen the truth behind the images, this prisoner can return and govern his still-deceived fellow prisoners. This story informs Plato's famous notion of the 'noble lie' that rulers are allowed to tell the populace in order to ensure their happiness. An earlier parable, the ring of Gyges, implicitly sets the stage, as it were, for this political theatre. In book two, one of Socrates' auditors, Plato's brother Glaucon, tells the story of a shepherd who discovers a gold ring that makes him invisible. Amazed by this power, the shepherd seduces the king's wife and then kills the king and takes over his position (Plato, 1991: 38). Although this story comes well before the discussions of mimesis, it suggests, much like the allegory of the cave, that political power lies in the control of images. Just as the invisible rulers of the cave use shadows to subdue the populace, so the shepherd uses his power over visibility to dethrone the king.

All of these examples suggest that Plato's theory of mimesis is very much a theory of political life. The imitator is not just a bad craftsman but a danger to the health of the republic; mimesis is not just a matter of stories and pictures but a problem for the nature of humanity itself. This claim often strikes modern readers as odd, but it is firmly grounded in the political context of Plato's age. Scholars have noted that Plato's exile of the poets is part of a larger debate in Greek culture over the respective place of poetry and philosophy in the education of the young and the conduct of public life, a debate clearly inflected in the dialogue by the highly patriarchal nature of this culture. As Eric Havelock has argued, Plato's criticisms imply that poetry held a monopoly over social and political life (1963: 36). Socrates himself refers at the end of his discussion of mimesis in book ten to 'an old quarrel between poetry and philosophy' (Plato, 1991: 290), and before he challenges the status of poetry near the end of the dialogue, he half-jokingly asks his auditors not to 'denounce me to the tragic poets and all the other imitators', as if they might see his argument as a power play (Plato, 1991: 277). The history of this struggle between poetry and philosophy, Havelock argues, arose out of a larger transition in the classical world from an oral to a literate culture. Prior to the fifth century BCE, Greek culture was maintained and transmitted by the rhapsodes who memorized and recited the great epics. Poetry was a repository of cultural wisdom, and the Greeks gave to Homeric epic in particular an authority and respect in public life far exceeding that which we accord to literature today. Much more than an ancient poet laureate, Homer was a cultural encyclopedia, offering the means of training leaders and providing models for civic virtue.

As Havelock suggests, the rise of writing during Plato's age had profound effects on the nature of knowledge. Although Plato often denounced writing (most famously in his dialogue the *Phaedrus*), and although the dialogues are staged as discussions, his philosophy is firmly grounded in the newly literate milieu. Preliterate cultures preserve communal knowledge largely through poetic techniques such as repetition, formulaic expressions, variations on familiar mythic paradigms, all of which aid memory. Such knowledge is founded on the interaction of speaker and auditor. Writing transforms knowledge into something visible, concrete and standardized. It makes possible precisely the emphasis on reason, calculation and conceptual analysis that characterizes Platonic philosophy. Socrates' exile of the poets in the *Republic*, Havelock argues, is part of a larger cultural struggle to assert the value of rigorous philosophical inquiry and literate culture over poetry and oral culture for contemporary Greek public life. The definition of poetry as mimesis is a conceptual revolution, a definitional *coup d'état*. Figured as secondary and derivative, distinguished from reason and truth and associated with femininity and childhood, poetry comes to seem inappropriate to the needs of current Greek society.

It is a technology of the past, limited to and by oral culture, and bound up with the interaction of mother and child rather than the political deliberation of mature men. It may be worthy of respect, but it is no longer suitable for new political realities.

2

ARISTOTLE'S *POETICS*

SECOND NATURE

Aristotle's *Poetics* is the single most influential work of literary criticism in the Western tradition and, along with Plato's *Republic*, is a foundational text for the understanding of mimesis. Very little is known about the origin and composition of the treatise, but it is most likely an incomplete or fragmentary compilation of lecture notes on tragic drama and related subjects, written sometime between 360 and 320 BCE, and probably addressed to and later compiled by students at Aristotle's school, the Lyceum, in Athens. The *Poetics* has long shaped critical accounts of ancient drama, and was treated by playwrights as a prescriptive guidebook for hundreds of years after its rediscovery and translation into Latin by scholars in the early Renaissance. Aristotle's chief subject is Greek tragedy, but his account of this form engages far-reaching questions about the nature of mimesis that powerfully revise Plato's theories. Aristotle's approach to mimesis is understated. What seem to be superficial assertions about narrative form or audience response are guided by sophisticated ideas about mimesis that, in many cases, have yet to be fully assimilated into contemporary popular discussions of art and literature.

Although it is often said that Aristotle's account of mimesis in the *Poetics* is a critical response to Plato's exile of the poets in the *Republic*, the relationship between the two philosophers is somewhat more complicated, and remains a matter of scholarly debate. Plato was Aristotle's teacher, and although he is never named in the treatise, his presence is unmistakable. Aristotle borrows a number of formulations from Plato, and challenges his teacher's claims about the nature and effects of mimesis, often in terms that seem directed against specific arguments Socrates makes in the *Republic*. Crucially, however, he does not question Plato's basic assertion that all art is essentially imitative. Even in his criticisms of Plato, Aristotle reinforces the conceptual hold of Platonic mimesis over Western art theory. Like Plato, Aristotle groups all the arts under the rubric of mimesis. And again like Plato, he contrasts the representational arts with other forms of human inquiry, such as science and history, that are conventionally associated with truth and reality. His defence of mimesis also turns on a fundamentally Platonic concern: reason. Aristotle counters Plato's assertion that mimesis is opposed to reason, and argues instead that tragedy offers quasi-philosophical insights into human actions. Mimesis, for Aristotle, is a real thing, worthy of critical analysis, but its definition still relies, like nearly all of the theories we shall discuss in this book, on the framework set up by Plato.

At the same time, Aristotle offers the most persuasive response to Plato's critique of mimesis. In many ways, the history of Western literary criticism is a repetition in different terms of the fundamental claims about mimesis in Plato and Aristotle. Unlike Plato, for whom mimesis is a mirror of something else and therefore potentially deceptive, Aristotle defines mimesis as a craft with its own internal laws and aims. The opening sentences of the *Poetics* establish this premise:

> I propose to treat of poetry in itself and of its various kinds, noting the essential quality of each; to inquire into the structure of the plot as requisite to a good poem; into the number and nature of the parts of which a poem is composed; and similarly into whatever else falls within the same inquiry. Following, then, the order of nature, let us begin with the principles which come first.
>
> (Aristotle, 1951: 7)

Aristotle says that he will treat poetry 'in itself', and not primarily as a reflection of something else. The poem, for Aristotle, is much like a natural object. We can study its parts and structure, classify it according to kind and aim, and determine in individual cases whether the object achieves its inherent objectives (whether it is 'good'). It is an appropriate subject for philosophical inquiry, which conforms to fixed principles and 'the order of nature'. Poetry might be said to imitate the processes of nature, and not just its physical forms.

Aristotle's metaphors for poetry throughout the *Poetics* stress the naturalness of mimesis. Whereas Plato's most common metaphors – mirrors, shadows, optical illusions – highlight the artificiality or unreality of art and literature, Aristotle's metaphors emphasize their similarity to natural objects. For example, in asserting that artistic beauty depends on the order and magnitude of the parts, Aristotle draws an analogy between art and animals: 'As, therefore, in the case of animate bodies and organisms, a certain magnitude is necessary' (1951: 31). Elsewhere, Aristotle compares the unity of plot to that of a body. Good plots 'resemble a living organism in all its unity, and produce the pleasure proper to it' (Aristotle, 1951: 89). In what might otherwise seem an extraneous or overly speculative discussion, Aristotle also offers a natural history of drama. Beginning in mere improvisation, and inspired by different aspects of Homeric epic, both tragedy and comedy developed according to the natural propensities of the poets drawn to each style. Serious poets wrote tragedies, while more frivolous ones turned to comedy. The development of tragedy, like that of an animal species, was governed by its inherent qualities: 'Having passed through many changes, it found its natural form, and there it stopped' (Aristotle, 1951: 19). Even the specific focus on tragic drama, which typically concerns troubled families, joins the definition of artistic genre to questions of biological gender and generation.

Aristotle's initial analysis of mimesis also embodies the argument that art has a specific nature of its own. The first three chapters of the *Poetics* differentiate what Aristotle calls the media, the objects and the manner of mimesis for the different representational arts. In each case, Aristotle borrows and modifies a distinction from Plato, or introduces a distinction where Plato fails to make one. The medium of imitation concerns the 'materials' each art uses to represent people and objects.

For Plato, poetry and painting, epic and tragedy are essentially the same in their imitation of the real. Aristotle, by contrast, differentiates the arts by the materials they employ. Painters use figure and colour, musicians melody and rhythm, dancers rhythm alone, and poets rhythm, language and melody. These arts are all mimetic, but they imitate with different tools, or use the same tools in different combinations. Rather than being a mere imitator, the artist is a maker, a craftsperson. Aristotle points out that many works use the same media as poetry does, but are not for that reason alone poems. Greek medical and scientific treatises were typically written in poetic metres, but the mere use of metre does not entitle the scientist to the name poet. It is, Aristotle argues, 'the imitation that makes the poet', not the rhetorical form of the work (Aristotle, 1951: 9). Although it is mimetic, then, poetry has its own proper methods and aims and is not just a diminished version of science or philosophy.

Aristotle offers a similar critique of Plato in his description of the objects of imitation. The objects that poetry depicts, he writes, are 'men in action' (Aristotle, 1951: 11). Aristotle takes this notion straight from Plato's discussion of tragedy in book ten of the *Republic*, but gives it a new interpretation. The individuals and actions depicted in art, he notes, are necessarily of a higher or lower moral type. While Plato treats such types according to their good or bad effect on the audience, Aristotle finds in the varying objects of mimesis a way of differentiating among genres and artistic styles. Each artist, and each artistic genre, emphasizes one human type and the actions appropriate to it. Epic and tragedy present people as better than they are in life, whereas comedy presents them as worse. Aristotle stresses that the moral standing of artistic subjects does not immediately affect the moral standing of the audience. Moral distinctions are markers of poetic genre, and cannot be unproblematically compared to moral distinctions in life. If mimesis can diverge from a strict reproduction of life, then it does far more than mirror the real.

The third difference that marks the various mimetic arts is the manner of imitation. Aristotle draws upon the distinction Socrates makes in book three of the *Republic* among forms of narration. Like Plato, Aristotle allows for three types of narration, but he modifies the categories. Poets can speak in their own voice (as in history), imitate the voice of the character (as in epic) or present the characters living and moving before the audience (as in drama). Aristotle's modification of Plato may seem minor, but it has far-reaching implications. Socrates treats the manner of imitation as a moral choice: the speaker who imitates another person 'hides' from the audience. Aristotle, by contrast, regards the manner of imitation as an artistic choice. The work can be narrated or performed, and the different forms of presentation are characteristic of different genres or artistic sensibilities. The manner of imitation, he suggests, should be judged not by whether it reveals or conceals the poet but by whether it is appropriate to the nature of the material. Although he is hardly an aesthete, Aristotle opens up the possibility, not fully explored until the nineteenth century, that artistic and ethical choices are distinct and should be kept separate.

Indeed, the careful distinction between art and ethics is a cornerstone of Aristotle's response to Plato. In a section of the *Poetics* devoted to formulating responses to certain unnamed 'critics' of poetry, Aristotle claims that the 'standard of correctness is not the same in poetry and politics, any more than in poetry and any other art' (Aristotle, 1951: 99). He distinguishes between 'essential' and 'accidental' errors in art. If a poet has imitated poorly or lacks skill, the error is essential. If, however, he or she has introduced 'technical inaccuracies' in the depiction of a craft, the error is accidental. It is far more important to imitate skilfully than to imitate exactly: 'not to know that a hind has no horns is a less serious matter than to paint it inartistically' (Aristotle, 1951: 99). Tellingly, Aristotle chooses the depiction of an animal (the hind, a female deer) to defend artists against their critics. If the work succeeds as art, he suggests, then it is not to be criticized for the factual failings that Plato attacks. Even the inclusion of impossible incidents can be justified 'if the end of the art be thereby attained' (Aristotle, 1951: 99). We should judge the success or failure of mimesis only in terms of its proper aims and methods, and not by a comparison with something else.

Aristotle also borrows, and effectively canonizes for later theorists, another key example from Plato: the behaviour of children. Plato regards the child's imitation as an instance of the broader dangers of mimesis. For Aristotle, children's imitations confirm the naturalness of mimesis. In an important passage from chapter four of the *Poetics*, he argues that poetry springs from two sources, 'each of them lying deep in our nature'.

First, mimesis is a natural capacity of all human beings, 'implanted in man from childhood', which distinguishes us from animals (Aristotle, 1951: 15). Humans are the most imitative of creatures, and we learn our earliest lessons through mimesis. Plato would most likely agree with this claim, but for Aristotle the association of mimesis with childhood points towards a broader claim about the value of art. As Stephen Halliwell has argued, Aristotle has in mind here the way children imaginatively act out adult behaviours and occupations (2002: 178). Such play has its own specific logic and developmental function, and does not simply ape what adults do, but fictionally recreates adult occupations. No one would fault children who play doctor for failing to cure the sick.

For Aristotle, as for Plato, children's play also provides a suggestive model for the way adults respond to mimetic works. Here again, he closely associates mimesis with the natural. This is the second 'source' of poetry. Like children, adults derive pleasure and knowledge from mimesis. Aristotle notes that we often gain pleasure in looking at representations of things that in themselves we find painful or repulsive, such as dead bodies or 'ignoble animals' (1951: 15). Mimesis provides fictional distance from things, so that the sufferings of tragic characters on stage can be pleasurable rather than painful, as they would be if they befell actual people. This fictional distance allows us to learn from representations, whereas we might respond emotionally to the actual experience. In this way, mimesis enables rational thought rather than, as Plato asserts, disabling it. Indeed, the pleasure of mimesis is closely tied to cognitive processes. Learning, Aristotle argues, is inherently pleasurable for all human beings, but mimesis allows for a particular kind of learning and pleasure: 'Thus the reason why men enjoy seeing a likeness is that in contemplating it they find themselves learning or inferring, and saying perhaps, "Ah, that is he"' (Aristotle, 1951: 15). At first glance, Aristotle seems to be suggesting that we simply compare the copy to the real thing, and gain pleasure through the comparison, but he is more likely arguing that mimesis provides insights into human action and character that we might not otherwise have. As he will argue later in the *Poetics*, mimesis concerns universals as well as particulars. The fictional distance inherent in mimesis allows a glimpse into the universal qualities of human life that are revealed by particular actions and characteristics. It teaches us what kind of person we are seeing on stage. Aristotle argues further that, even if we have not seen the original, we still can still gain pleasure from 'the execution, the coloring, or some such other cause' (1951: 15). The material form of mimesis is part of what makes it both enjoyable and potentially educational.

TRAGEDY, PLOT AND REASON

As we have seen, Aristotle borrows many details in his account of mimesis from the *Republic*, but greatly complicates and revalues Plato's ideas. Aristotle stresses that mimesis, far from being an alien intruder in the otherwise harmonious soul, is in fact a natural aspect of human life, and even a unique source of learning. His use of organic metaphors and the example of childhood play reinforces the claim that mimesis need not be a threat to the soul or the city. We find a similar effort to revalue Plato's judgements in Aristotle's account of tragedy. Plato argues that tragedy dangerously stirs our emotions at the expense of our rational faculties. For Aristotle, tragedy is soundly rational. Indeed, although tragedy often deals with extreme emotions, irrational desires and supernatural forces, good tragedies are constructed rationally and engage the rational faculties of the audience. Even tragic emotions, Aristotle argues, can be made predictable and reasonable.

Aristotle begins his discussion of tragedy with a definition:

> Tragedy, then, is an imitation of an action that is serious, complete, and of a certain magnitude; in language embellished with each kind of artistic ornament, the several kinds being found in separate parts of the play; in the form of action not narrative; through pity and fear effecting the purgation of these emotions.
>
> (1951: 23)

All tragedies have six parts: plot (*mythos*), character (*ethos*), diction (*lexis*), thought (*dianoia*), spectacle (*opsis*) and song (*melopoeia*). Plot is the arrangement of incidents; character is the particular moral qualities of the agents revealed by the plot; diction is the metrical arrangement of words; thought is the process of reasoning that characters use to defend or justify themselves; spectacle is the stage machinery; and song refers to the musical passages that were common in Greek tragedy. As is typical with Aristotle, what initially seem banal and rather dry distinctions turn out to be complicated and far-reaching in implication. On one level, this definition simply categorizes tragedy as a form of mimesis: its medium is language and rhythm (diction, song); its objects are men and actions (plot, character, thought); and it is performed rather than narrated (spectacle). On another level, though, the definition proposes a comprehensive theory about the nature of tragedy and the rationality of mimesis.

There is a great deal to be said about each of these terms, but for our purposes we can attend primarily to plot. Let us begin with the first two parts of Aristotle's initial definition: that tragedy is the mimesis of an action and that this action is complete and of a certain magnitude. Completeness, for Aristotle, does not refer to a subjective sense of resolution but to the structural relationship of incidents:

> A whole is that which has a beginning, a middle, and an end. A beginning is that which does not itself follow anything by causal necessity, but after which something naturally is or comes to be. An end, on the contrary, is that which itself naturally follows some other thing, either by necessity or as a rule, but has nothing following it. A middle is that which follows something as some other thing follows it.
>
> (Aristotle, 1951: 31)

While this passage might seem to border on tautology, Aristotle is making a major claim about mimesis. Simply describing an artwork as whole and complete flies in the face of Plato's claim that mimesis is dependent on something else and hence by definition incomplete. For Aristotle, the mimetic work can have its own internal unity, a unity governed by necessity and reason, not by chance, deception or individual whim. Beginning, middle and end are logical categories, not just temporal markers. The beginning causes something to happen, sets a chain of events in motion; the middle is caused by the beginning, and causes something else in turn; and an end is produced 'by necessity or as a rule' out of something else, but has no consequences of its own. One could define the principles of physics or of bodily functions in much the same terms. Reason and law are the foundation of mimesis, even if the story itself concerns lawless acts or emotional extremes.

A similar stress on rationality informs Aristotle's account of magnitude. Beauty, Aristotle claims, relies on both order (that is, completeness) and magnitude. While order is defined logically, magnitude is defined in terms of the audience and, more specifically, in terms of human cognitive processes. If order describes the rational relationship among the parts of a tragedy, magnitude describes the processes by which the audience discerns this relationship:

> a very small animal organism cannot be beautiful; for the view of it is confused, the object being seen in an almost imperceptible moment of time. Nor again can one of vast size be beautiful; for as the eye cannot take it all in at once, the unity and sense of the whole is lost for the spectator.
>
> (Aristotle, 1951: 31)

Smallness or largeness are not absolute qualities, but reflect the position and cognitive abilities of the viewer. A work has proper magnitude, conveys beauty and a sense of unity, if the spectator can grasp it in one view. 'Seeing' here, as elsewhere in Aristotle and Plato, is a key metaphor for knowing. The single 'view' refers to a single train of thought. The sense of unity we gain from a mimetic work is defined by the unity of the thought process it inspires. Thus the proper magnitude for a tragedy is 'a length which can be easily embraced by the memory' (Aristotle, 1951: 33).

Aristotle's emphasis on the rationality of mimesis explains his focus throughout the *Poetics* on plot. Aristotle claims that plot is the single most important element of tragedy: it is, he says, the 'soul [*psyche*]' of a tragedy, the very seat of its rational faculties (1951: 29). We are now more accustomed to understanding character as the key to literary art, but Aristotle ranks plot higher, chiefly because it is only through actions and choices that character is revealed. Action, for Aristotle, is a basic unit of human understanding. But even more crucially, plot epitomizes the rationality of tragic mimesis. Plot is not simply a mimesis of action but of action ordered and structured to achieve certain ends. Unlike the theatrical staging associated with spectacle, which Aristotle sees as irrational, plot is governed by reason. The incidents in a tragic plot should be unified by probability and necessity. Such unity does not come from the focus on a single character, since an individual's life may contain many different plots. Nor can a single historical period or mythic tale be made without selection and reordering into a unified plot. Aristotle points to the example of Homer, who bases the *Iliad* on a major turn of events in the Trojan war, not on the entire conflict. The worst plots are episodic, where the events seem simply to follow one another in time, and not by any internal logic. Unlike good tragic plots, such episodic plots are not unified by probability and necessity and therefore do not appeal to reason.

Aristotle's focus on probability and necessity suggests that the realism of a mimetic work comes not from its reflection of the external world but from its congruence with the norms of human thought. The work strikes us as realistic because the events of the plot are joined according to the same rules that govern events in our actual experience. Reasoning in and about art is not essentially different from reasoning in other contexts. As in art, so in daily life we rely on logic (necessity) and belief (probability) in making choices. Mimetic artists are thus perfectly justified in seeking validation for their artistic choices in other places than brute fact. They might appeal to the example of Sophocles, who depicted people as better than they are, and claim that their art aims for higher truths. Or they might appeal to custom or received opinion – 'what is said' (Aristotle, 1951: 101) – even if those opinions are manifestly false from the perspective of philosophy. By the same token, unfamiliar or impossible actions can be plausible if they resonate with habitual manners of thinking. Aristotle notes, for example, that impossible incidents can be made realistic if they seem probable. Indeed, such incidents may be artistically preferable to the truth, so long as they are called for by the 'inner necessity' of the work: 'a probable impossibility is to be preferred to a thing improbable and yet possible' (Aristotle, 1951: 107). The effect of the work comes from the rational ordering of events, not from the realistic quality of the individual events the play represents. Even though Aristotle counsels the poet against including irrational events, he nevertheless acknowledges that, from an artistic perspective, the irrational 'sometimes does not violate reason' (1951: 107). Mimesis, in other words, need not be true to fact to be pleasurable and persuasive. It need only be true to the principles and normal processes of human cognition.

Aristotle also argues that the tragic action should adhere to reason and the norms of human cognition. This dictate applies both to the structure of the plot and to the behaviour of the main characters. Aristotle divides plots into two kinds – the simple and the complex. Simple plots are one and continuous, detailing, for example, the steady decline of a character's fortunes through a closely linked series of events, whereas complex plots are marked by a reversal and recognition. Reversals (*peripeteia*) occur when an action veers around to its opposite. Aristotle gives the example of a royal messenger in Sophocles' tragedy *Oedipus the King* (*c*.426 BCE), who comes to give Oedipus the good news that he has become the king of Corinth, but instead accidentally reveals disturbing details about his origins. Recognition (*anagnorisis*) describes a character's change from ignorance to knowledge, which produces love or hate between persons or marks a change of fortune. Both reversal and recognition are grounded in reason. Reversals, for example, 'should arise from the internal structure of the plot, so that what follows should be the necessary or probable result of the preceding action' (Aristotle, 1951: 39, 41). Reversals that do not adhere to these laws will strike the viewer as arbitrary and unconvincing. Recognition also describes a rational process. Here the character reasons and draws inferences from various kinds of evidence, such as suspicious objects or other people. In both structure and unfolding, then, tragic plots rely upon, and inspire, a cognitive effort on the part of poet, characters and audience.

Indeed, poetry approaches the status of philosophy for Aristotle. Against Plato's claim that there is an ancient war between poetry and philosophy, Aristotle argues that poets, somewhat like philosophers, concern themselves with universal principles of action and character and not with mere fact. More than simply imitating what is or has been, poets relate 'what may happen' according to probability and necessity, or what is broadly and characteristically true of a given type of situation (1951: 35). Historians, by contrast, are limited to what has happened. This makes poetry a higher pursuit than history. The historian expresses the particular, and remains tied to facts. The poet, by contrast, expresses the universal by way of particular characters or actions: 'how a person of a certain type will on occasion speak or act, according to the law of probability and necessity' (Aristotle, 1951: 35). Thus poetry is 'more philosophical' than history. This is true even when the poet takes a historical subject. The poet, Aristotle writes, is 'the maker of plots rather than of verses' (1951: 37). Aristotle again condenses a major point into an unassuming comparison. Mimesis is defined not by its repetition of the real but by its ability to reveal universal truths in particular characters and actions. While Plato sees the poet's divergence from fact as a key failure, Aristotle regards it as part of the poet's most characteristic power. History, bound as it is to repeating facts, comes closer to Plato's account of mimesis than poetry does.

THE TRAGIC EFFECT

Aristotle extends his claim that mimesis is rational to his account of the ways in which tragedy affects its audience. Although the tragic effect is fundamentally emotional, the particular emotions Aristotle identifies, and the process by which the poet produces them in the spectator, are entirely rational. Unlike Plato, Aristotle does not simply oppose the emotions to reason, nor does he insist that tragedy's ability to rouse the emotions threatens to destabilize the city and the soul. For Aristotle, emotion is the proper issue of tragic mimesis, not its problematic side effect. Such response is predictable, closely tied to the development of the plot, and can be managed by the poet. Poets fail when they do not produce tragic emotions – not, as for Plato, when they do. Thus Aristotle explains how tragic poets can best produce the 'essential tragic effect' (1951: 29), and suggests that tragedy's power to rouse the emotions, far from being a danger to the spectator, is a natural and rational response to mimesis. The particular emotions Aristotle identifies are produced by both identification and reflection on the part of the spectator. The end result of these emotions is not more emotion, as Plato insists, but a release or refinement of emotion, and a consequent improvement of the spectator's emotional state.

According to Aristotle, tragic emotions are a result of the plot structure as a whole, and not just a catastrophic event at the end. They are most effectively produced in the audience by surprising turns of events. But surprise is only effective if it seems to issue from the causal logic of the plot: 'The tragic wonder will then be greater than if they happened of themselves or by accident; for even coincidences are most striking when they have an air of design' (Aristotle, 1951: 39). Even the most horrifying event will seem arbitrary, and thus fail to elicit the proper emotions, if it strikes the audience as improbable. Aristotle gives the example of the statue of Mitys at Argos, which, according to legend, fell on and killed the man who murdered Mitys. Although the incident seems to arise out of mere chance or by way of irrational forces, it has what Aristotle calls an 'air of design': even though the coincidence seems supernaturally motivated, it is internally logical, and so satisfies our sense of probability and necessity. Aristotle further suggests that the true tragic pleasure should arise not from the spectacle, but from the inner structure of the plot: 'For the plot ought to be so constructed that, even without the aid of the eye, he who hears the tale told will thrill with horror and melt with pity at what takes place' (1951: 49). Emotions produced by spectacle alone, such as frightening masks or special effects, will engender a sense of the monstrous and not of the feelings proper to tragedy. Such emotions are irrational, and 'within the action there must be nothing irrational' (Aristotle, 1951: 57).

Aristotle identifies two essential tragic emotions: fear (*phobos*) and pity (*eleos*). Pity is aroused by unmerited misfortune, and fear by 'the misfortune of a man like ourselves' (Aristotle, 1951: 45). Both of these emotions presuppose a complex cognitive process. Whereas Plato imagines emotion in the audience as an imitation of the emotions depicted on the stage, Aristotle describes a form of psychological identification. The effects of fear and pity that we experience in the theatre, while genuine, differ from the effects of these emotions in daily life. In other contexts, we might run from something we fear, or offer help to an object of pity. Yet much as mimesis allows us to view dead bodies dispassionately, so it also allows us to experience our emotions dispassionately, to enjoy them rather than suffer from or react to them. Aristotle never explicitly describes this process, but he clearly associates tragic emotion with the same cognitive processes that define our response to plot more generally. Even in the grip of emotion, the spectators reflect upon the actions of the tragic character, and compare the character with themselves. Only certain situations rouse tragic fear and pity. We do not feel pity for every misfortune, but only for those that come to people who do not deserve it. We must therefore have a sense of what would be probable in order to discern an unmerited misfortune. Similarly, we feel fear only when we can relate what befalls the tragic character to the circumstances of our own lives. We implicitly compare ourselves with the character, and imaginatively put ourselves in his or her place. Much as pity demands both sympathy and moral judgement, so fear demands imagination and self-reflection. Mimesis allows us a form of distance that enables rational reflection on even disturbing sights, and tragedy in particular produces emotional effects out of a rational reflection on the course of human life.

Aristotle's detailed account of how mimesis affects our emotions stands in notable contrast to Plato's suspicion of all tragic emotions. Whereas Plato sets emotion and reason in opposition, Aristotle suggests that tragedy produces emotions rationally, and that the key tragic emotions are themselves grounded in reason. Aristotle also challenges Plato's account of the emotions roused by mimesis in his controversial claim about the ultimate effect of tragedy for the audience. Plato argues that mimesis arouses emotions that would best be suppressed. Aristotle claims, by contrast, that tragedy can lead to the 'purgation' (*katharsis*) of the emotions. This is the final clause of his initial definition of tragedy: 'through pity and fear effecting the proper purgation of these emotions' (Aristotle, 1951: 23).

There are few passages in the history of literary theory that have produced as much debate and speculation as this so-called 'catharsis clause'. On the most basic level, Aristotle seems to be arguing that tragedy does not simply arouse emotions but allows for their beneficial release or transformation. Tragedy is broadly therapeutic rather than pathological, allowing us to experience fears or fantasies vicariously so that we do not need to enact them in life. But this is where uncertainty sets in. Part of the difficulty of understanding this clause lies in the many meanings and uses of the word catharsis in Greek culture. Each meaning suggests a different account of the function of tragic mimesis. Etymologically, catharsis means to prune or cut away. Plato often uses some derivative of the word to describe the way philosophical dialogue removes our incorrect opinions. Accordingly, some scholars have suggested that Aristotle imagines catharsis as a kind of 'intellectual clarification' (Golden, 1992). Eighteenth-century theorists, by contrast, understood the purifying effect of catharsis as a form of moral improvement. The German critic and playwright G. E. Lessing, for example, argues in his *Hamburg Dramaturgy* (1767–69) that tragic catharsis brings about 'the transformation of passions into virtuous habits' (1962: 193). Tragedy makes us better citizens by making us more humble and sympathetic.

But other contexts for the word go against this notion. The most common uses of the word catharsis in ancient Greece described a ritual purification or a medical purge. The notion of purification suggests that tragedy improves us either by washing away our problematic emotions or by purifying the emotions themselves. The medical definition would claim that tragedy literally purges us of unhealthful feelings. This interpretation, first proposed by Jacob Bernays in 1857, was important for modern interpreters, notably Bernays' nephew by marriage, Sigmund Freud. But the purgative account sits uneasily with Aristotle's claim that tragedy is both pleasurable and intellectually illuminating. Construing Aristotle's syntax differently raises another question: does tragedy purge existing emotions, those the audience members bring with them to the theatre, or does it purge emotions that it arouses? The various meanings of word of catharsis seem to suggest the former, but the attention Aristotle gives to fear and pity points us to the latter. In this reading, tragedy would provide a kind of emotional purgation by rousing fear and pity and allowing us to enjoy them, not by removing the fear and pity we bring to the theatre or by altering our general emotional state. Catharsis would describe the proper result of the tragic plot. In a suggestive reworking of this reading, the twentieth-century French playwright Antonin Artaud reimagines theatre as a plague that brings forth 'all the perverse possibilities of the mind' (1958: 30). For Artaud, the aim of catharsis is metaphorically to sicken the audience, not to cure it.

These disputes over the meaning of catharsis are unlikely to be answered in any definitive way. But this should not distract us from the originality of Aristotle's conception. Although Aristotle canonizes Plato's reduction of all art to mimesis, he also provides what remains the most powerful defence of art in the history of literary theory. Alongside the claim that mimesis is natural, rational and educational, the notion of catharsis implies that art might also be beneficial. In his acknowledgement that it is secondary and derivative, Aristotle gives art a primary and crucial function. The effects of this double argument continue to resonate in current discussions of art.

PART TWO

Three Versions of Mimesis

3

IMITATIO
Rhetorical Imitation

MIMESIS AS A CULTURAL PRACTICE

As we saw in the last two chapters, the theory of mimesis in Plato and Aristotle forges a powerful link between human behaviour and artistic representation. Far more than an account of how art mirrors nature, mimesis entails a complicated set of ideas about how human beings think, feel and understand the world and each other. The next three chapters will trace the influence of these ideas over two millennia of Western theory, and across the various fine arts. In particular, we will be discussing the three most common and important elements in the thematic complex of mimesis: the imitation of role models; the imagery of theatre and acting; and the problem of realism. These elements provide three pivotal ways in which mimesis can be defined and described. The imitation of role models concerns the relationship between past and present, original and copy, and defines mimesis as a historical phenomenon. Theatre, by contrast, emphasizes the relationship between the work and its audience, and defines mimesis by its presentation and effects. Realism, finally, concerns the relationship between work and world, and defines mimesis by its more or less accurate reproduction of nature. In each case, these relationships are governed by social and artistic conventions that in large part determine whether a literary, artistic or theatrical work strikes us as mimetic. As we shall find, the definition of mimesis is remarkably flexible, and changes greatly over time and across cultural contexts.

My topic for this chapter is the phenomenon of rhetorical imitation, the imitation of artistic role models, which, for the long stretch of Western history between the height of the Roman empire and the end of the eighteenth century, was a central principle of literary production. In addition to imitating nature and human action, poets also actively sought to imitate exemplary forerunners and the artistic conventions they made authoritative. This theory was designated by the word ancient Latin writers used to translate the Greek term mimesis: *imitatio*. The key to literary success, it was argued, was the skilful imitation of role models and the ability to make something new out of old traditions. In his verse treatise 'An Essay on Criticism' (1711), the English poet Alexander Pope offers an influential summary of this version of mimesis. Perhaps unsurprisingly, Pope's first and most important rule for the poet is to 'follow nature'. But his sense of nature turns out to be quite distinct:

> Unerring nature! Still divinely bright,
> One clear, unchanged, and universal light,
> Life, force, and beauty, must to all impart,
> At once the source, and end, and test of art.
>
> (Pope, 1971: ll. 70–3)

On the surface, this claim seems to resonate with the familiar notion of art that we encountered in Plato and Aristotle. Yet for Pope, artists should not seek directly to imitate the physical world or human actions but should instead look to the exemplary artworks handed down from antiquity for guidance. Raw nature is too wild and unruly for proper imitation. The ancient works Pope encourages the poet to follow, by contrast, are 'nature methodized' (Pope, 1971: l. 89). They teach a proven set of rules for the representation of nature, rules that encourage lawfulness and restraint. Pope is not arguing for self-conscious artificiality, since the rules of art are a formalized version of nature itself. The way to the true imitation of nature, in other words, goes through art and tradition: 'Learn hence for ancient rules a just esteem; / To copy nature is to copy them' (Pope, 1971: ll. 139–40). Pope offers the example of the ancient Roman epic poet Virgil (70–19 BCE), who found the proper form for his own work by imitating another author: 'Nature and Homer were, he found, the same' (Pope, 1971: l. 135). Both nature and Homer teach restraint and design, lessons that are better learned in literature than in the landscape. Following nature, in this instance, does not mean trusting instinct or describing flowers. It means following the best human role models and imitating trusted conventions.

Pope's assertion that great art comes from the imitation of role models and not from the untutored mirroring of nature is poised at the end of a critical tradition that dominated the literary and intellectual culture of Europe for nearly two thousand years. As we shall see at the end of this chapter, this version of mimesis was vigorously challenged by theorists in the late eighteenth century, who argued that imitation is mechanical, unoriginal, even plagiaristic. Yet this belief, which we continue to share with these theorists, is itself based on a rather mechanical reassertion of the Platonic paradigm of copy and original: the imitation is a mere copy of the true original. At its height, however, the theory and practice of imitating role models powerfully reconfigured this paradigm by making the process of imitation an integral part of the artwork rather than just its anthropological origin. Indeed, there is nothing inherently uncreative about the practice of *imitatio*, which is responsible for some of the central works of Western art and literature. Artists and audiences from antiquity to the eighteenth century found artistic pleasure in the reconfiguration of traditional materials, in old stories made fresh, in reassuring confirmations of accepted truths, and in the surprising use of a familiar convention. This is true of Pope's own statement of his doctrines. In pointing to a prominent instance of literary imitation (Virgil and Homer), Pope gives voice to the commonplace belief that artists should serve an apprenticeship to the classics. One finds similar advice in theoretical works from ancient Rome to eighteenth-century England and Germany. Indeed, Pope's treatise is an imitation of another influential verse treatise, the *Ars Poetica*, written more than seventeen hundred years earlier by one of Pope's literary models, the

Roman poet Horace. Like Pope, Horace counsels imitation: 'Study Greek models day and night' (Russell and Winterbottom, 1972: 286). Pope's theoretical claim both advocates and practices *imitatio*.

With its turn toward an illustrious past, literary imitation was an indispensable mechanism for cultural stability and a powerful means of asserting the unity of contemporary culture with the past. This process was often described as a *translatio studii*: the carrying over of learning from one culture to another. The Romans laid claim to Greek tradition by imitating Greek art, and European writers in the Renaissance asserted a continuity with classical antiquity by imitating the Romans. Classical literary genres first became classical through imitation. Epic, pastoral, comedy and tragedy all originated in Greece, probably arising out of ritual and ceremonial contexts. They became recognizable as literary forms because they were objects of imitation, first by later generations of Greek writers and then by the Romans. Virgil imitated the pastoral poetry of Theocritus; Horace imitated the odes of Pindar; Ovid rewrote Greek myths; Plautus and Terence imitated the comedies of Aristophanes; Seneca retold the tragic narratives of Sophocles. Although we tend to think of these genres as eternal and immutable, they are the historical products of imitation. There is, in this regard, a critical and creative aspect to *imitatio*. Imitation makes the original an original, renders it a 'classic' and a model for further imitation. Far from simply echoing the greater forerunner, imitation transforms the original into a recognizable set of conventions. Imitation is the effective origin of tradition itself.

Perhaps the best example of such generic imitation is the epic. Virgil's *Aeneid* (19 BCE) tells of the origins of the Roman empire out of the fall of Troy but, as Pope noted, this story has its own origins in Homer's two epics, the *Iliad* and the *Odyssey*. Virgil builds his story out of the subjects of these epics (the fall of Troy and the wanderings of Odysseus), and borrows many of Homer's characters. He also adopts the structure of Homeric epics: where Homer's works are each composed in twenty-four books, Virgil composed his in twelve. Virgil places key episodes in his epic with this structural parallel in mind. For example, Homer's hero Odysseus undertakes a *catabasis* (descent to the underworld) at the middle of the *Odyssey*, while Virgil's hero Aeneas makes his own descent at the middle (book six) of the *Aeneid*. Virgil's placement of the epic *catabasis* became a touchstone for later writers of epic. John Milton narrates one version of Satan's fall from heaven to hell in book six of *Paradise Lost* (1667). And in chapter six of *Ulysses* (1922), James Joyce's modern-day Odysseus, Leopold Bloom, attends a funeral. There is nothing inherently epic about a descent to the underworld, or about the number six. Both gain significance through Virgil's imitation of Homer, and the subsequent imitations of writers from Dante to Joyce. The epic underworld, as scholars have noted, is a scene of *imitatio*: a place where the hero speaks with his forerunners, and where epic poets join their work to a tradition. Indeed, the medieval Italian poet Dante is led through hell by Virgil in *The Inferno* (1314).

It would be inaccurate to see *imitatio* as a mere defence of rigid conformity or deference to the past, though. *Imitatio* takes many different forms in Roman and Renaissance literature, from verbal echoes and allusions to full-scale rewritings of prior works, translations, imaginary dialogues with ancient authorities, even parodic overturnings of classical ideals. As Thomas Greene writes, moreover, '[t]he process called imitation was not only a technique or a habit; it was also a field of ambivalence, drawing together manifold, tangled, sometimes antithetical attitudes, hopes, pieties, and reluctances within a concrete locus' (1982: 45). As every school child knows, imitation can be cruel as well as complimentary. Students imitate their teachers and friends out of respect, but also to mock or subvert. This double quality of imitation is no less true of Roman and Renaissance literary culture than it is of the schoolyard. Writers struggled with a sense of rivalry, belatedness and even hostility towards their role models. Dante and Milton imitate the form of Virgilian epic, but also contrast their Christian ideals with what they consider to be the limited moral universe of pagan antiquity. Thus, for example, the character in *Paradise Lost* who most resembles Aeneas is Satan. Parody and satire are also based on imitation, and gain their edge by modelling themselves on recognizable styles or social types. We laugh at a parody because we know the original, and can discern the ways in which the copy subtly diverges from it. No less than epic, parody relies upon the practice of *imitatio*.

As these examples suggest, the tradition of *imitatio* anticipates what literary theorists have called intertextuality, the notion that all cultural products are a tissue of narratives and images borrowed from a familiar storehouse. Art absorbs and manipulates these narratives and images rather than creating anything wholly new. From ancient Greece to the beginnings of Romanticism, familiar stories and images circulated throughout Western culture, often anonymously. One of the great works of Renaissance scholarship, the *Adages* of the sixteenth-century Dutch humanist Erasmus, was a sprawling collection of, and learned commentary upon, thousands of classical proverbs. This collection was intended to give writers a sure footing in their own use of familiar material. It sought to enable a *translatio studii* of ancient wisdom into the European vernaculars. The project implies that all writing is a more or less conscious imitation of available cultural materials. Many areas of contemporary culture conform to this notion, despite our post-Romantic disdain of imitation. Both television sitcoms and popular music, for example, work within very restricted forms, and concern a limited number of familiar situations. Hip-hop songs even incorporate actual bits and pieces from earlier songs. Fashion, to take another example, nearly always alludes to past styles while also adding something new to its design. The originality of a sitcom, a pop song or a new fashion, much like the deployment of a proverb for Erasmus, is measured not by its absolute uniqueness but by its creative use of existing ideas and conventions.

ROMAN ECHOES

It is often said that Rome conquered Greece politically, only to be conquered in turn by Greek art and culture. A great deal of Roman art and literature borrow their form and subject matter from Greek sources, and it is almost impossible to understand Roman literary culture without reference to the concept of *imitatio*. If mimesis originates in Greece, it gains its most enduring form in this pervasive Roman practice. *Imitatio* was central to Roman literary education, and was regarded as an essential method for artistic innovation. The question for any Roman poet was not whether to imitate but how best to do it. *Imitatio* was also a historical and political practice. Roman artists saw themselves not just as imitators of Greek models but as heirs to Greek tradition. Nor did they imitate simply to praise the Greeks but also to surpass their models, to invest Greek forms with an ideal of Roman virtue. As G. M. A. Grube writes, Roman writers 'deliberately set out to forge their own language into an instrument by means of which they could hope to rival the Greeks with masterpieces of their own' (1965: 153).

Horace's ode on the ancient Greek lyric poet Pindar, probably written around 13 BCE, offers a suggestive example of this cultural dynamic. Horace imitates Pindar, but forges something new with his poetic material. The ode, addressed to Mark Antony's second son, Iulus Antonius, opens with a suggestion that imitating Pindar is hubristic:

> Whoever strives to rival Pindar,
> O Iulus, is flying on wings
> fastened with wax by Daedalean artifice
> destined to lend
>
> his name to a crystal sea.
>
> (Horace, 1999: 155)

Like the mythical Icarus, who flew too close to the sun with wax wings made by his father, Daedalus, and fell to his death in the Icarian Sea, the poet who tries to rival Pindar on his own terms is bound to fail. Horace compares Pindar to a rain-swollen river, and suggests that he was an eye-witness to the acts of gods and heroes. As the poem develops, though, the wings of Icarus are subtly transformed:

> I instead, so small, so humble,
> after the manner and the art
> of the Matinian bee,
>
> who, assiduously toiling
> in the groves and along the banks of the humid Tiber
> gathers the pleasant thyme,
> So do I
>
> fashion my elaborately worked verses.
>
> (Horace, 1999: 156)

At first glance, Horace seems to say that he is a mere honey bee, a laborious craftsman rather than an uncontainable and quasi-divine force of nature, and thus no match for his role model. But while bees are small and industrious, they have the ability to transform nature. They use nature (flowers) in order to create honey and wax. Honey does not 'imitate' flowers, but draws upon their essence, much as Horace himself draws upon Pindar, to make something new, useful and pleasurable. Bees are an image of culture within nature, and a metaphor for the way Horace tames the wild Pindar and makes him into a model for other poets. Wax is also a metaphor for *imitatio*. Much as wax can change its shape without changing its essence, so Horace transforms Pindar without simply repeating him. Horace thus differentiates two kinds of imitation: while rejecting a slavish imitation (Icarus' fatal imitation of the birds), he argues for a more powerful idea of imitation as transformation (the bee's production of honey and wax).

The most explicit discussions of *imitatio* in Roman discourse are found in rhetorical manuals and theoretical treatises from the era. Nearly all of the major orators from the period discuss imitation, and often echo Horace in treating it not as a mere repetition but as a critical practice that demands all of the imitator's literary skill and judgement. In one of the earliest known discussions of *imitatio* from the period, the Greek orator Dionysius of Halicarnassus (first century BCE) contrasts these two forms of imitation:

> An imitation is related to the ancient models in two different ways: the first relationship is the natural result of being for a long time in close contact with the model and living with it, the second resembles it but results from the application of rhetorical rules. About the first kind there is little one can say, about the second one can say only that all the models have a natural grace and charm of their own, while their contrived imitations, even if they are as perfect as imitations can be, always have something laboured or unnatural about them.
>
> (Quoted in Grube, 1965: 211–12)

Like Horace, Dionysius argues for a practice of *imitatio* closer to emulation (the Greek *zelos* and Latin *aemulatio*) than to copying. He insists that imitations should reproduce the 'natural grace and charm' of the model, not just its verbal and stylistic features. Writing more than one hundred years later, the rhetorician Quintilian would echo this sentiment in his influential discussion of imitation in the *Institutio Oratoria*

(Education of the Orator), published in 95 CE. Quintilian argues that *imitatio* is a crucial part of the orator's training, but that the imitator needs to possess a critical awareness of what makes a speech worthy as a model: 'it is the first essential that everyone should understand what he is proposing to imitate and why it is good' (Russell and Winterbottom, 1972: 402). Yet what makes a speech worthy of imitation is also what imitation cannot provide: 'the greatest qualities of an orator – talent, facility of discovery, force, fluency, everything that art cannot supply – these things are not imitable'. Thus imitators should be 'rivals, not followers' of those they take as role models (Russell and Winterbottom, 1972: 401).

Roman authors often dwelled on the difference between imitation and emulation, between mere copying and rivalry or transformation. One of the most important discussions of imitation in Roman literature is by the philosopher Seneca (4 BCE to 65 CE). In his *Epistle 84*, Seneca offers his young correspondent Lucilius advice on reading. Drawing upon the same honey bee metaphor Horace uses in describing his imitation of Pindar, Seneca offers an elegant formulation of a key Roman belief about imitation, that one should draw inspiration from many different sources, not just one: 'We should follow, men say, the example of the bees, who flit about and cull the flowers that are suitable for producing honey, and then arrange and assort in their cells all that they have brought in' (Seneca, 1920: 277). Like good imitators, bees improve upon their sources by selection and arrangement, as well as by transformation. Writers collect many different ideas, learn from many different role models, selecting what is valuable and arranging it into something new. The resulting product draws upon the virtues of the models but also transforms them, much as bees turn flowers into honey and wax: 'we should so blend those several flavors into one delicious compound that, even though it betrays its origin, yet it nevertheless is clearly a different thing from whence it came' (Seneca, 1920: 279). The best imitation, Seneca argues, will both resemble and differ from its sources. Seneca compares this transformative power of good imitation to digestion, where different foods are assimilated for the benefit of the body, and to a chorus, where each individual voice is combined with others to produce a new unity. He also compares it to the resemblance between a parent and a child:

> Even if there shall appear in you a likeness to him who, by reason of your admiration, has left a deep impress upon you, I would have you resemble him as a child resembles his father, and not as a picture resembles its original; for a picture is a lifeless thing.
>
> (Seneca, 1920: 281)

Unlike a picture, which aims for an accurate mimesis of appearances, children resemble their parents without merely copying them. Children have their own tastes and personalities, grow and develop, and can in turn become parents of another child. Good imitators, for Seneca, might be said to choose their own parents: they come to resemble a model out of admiration, but not slavish devotion.

One of the most important documents of ancient literary criticism, and the source for another key account of *imitatio*, is 'On the Sublime', written sometime in the first century CE. This treatise is traditionally attributed to 'Longinus', about whom little is known. Written in Greek, it offers a reflection on literary techniques for producing sublimity, which Longinus defines as a sense of wonder and astonishment we gain from writing that goes beyond mere persuasion. Among these techniques is the imitation of role models. But whereas most rhetorical theorists treat imitation as an educational practice, Longinus compares it to spiritual possession:

> It is like what we are told of the Pythia at Delphi: she is in contact with the tripod near the cleft in the ground which (so they say) exhales a divine vapour, and she is thereupon made pregnant by the supernatural power and forthwith prophesies as one inspired. Similarly, the genius of the ancients acts as a kind of oracular cavern, and effluences flow from it into the minds of their imitators. Even those previously not much inclined to prophesy become inspired and share the enthusiasm which comes from the greatness of others.
>
> (Russell and Winterbottom, 1972: 476)

The original, for Longinus, is akin to a divine force that possesses and 'impregnates' the imitator. Imitation feminizes the belated follower. And yet, the divine forerunner also depends upon the human imitator. It is the follower alone, such as the Pythia at Delphi, who can make the past speak to humans. The metaphor of impregnation places true creativity in the follower. Without this follower, the spirit of the past would remain obscure, trapped in the cave and without a human voice.

ANCIENTS AND MODERNS

These examples highlight the richness of Roman theories of *imitatio*. Rather than urging a stereotypically slavish reliance on a role model, writers such as Horace, Seneca and Longinus offer subtle accounts of how artists relate to the past and create something new through mimesis. For Renaissance writers of the fourteenth, fifteenth and sixteenth centuries, the entire Roman tradition itself stands at once as an inimitable example, a continuing ideal of literary practice and a dangerous rival. Although the Roman past held great authority for Renaissance artists and scholars, it was also associated with a hostile religion and unfamiliar social practices. It was a problematic model for devout Christian writers. Something of the complexity of this relation can be found in one of the key medieval statements about *imitatio*, by the twelfth-century author Pierre de Blois. Responding in a letter to criticism of his interest in the ancients, he defends the *imitatio* with what would become a famous metaphor:

> We are like dwarfs mounted on the shoulders of giants; with their assistance we can see further than they can; clinging to their works, we restore a new life to their more elegant thoughts, which time or the neglect of men had already left dead.
>
> (Quoted in Greene, 1982: 84)

Although the ancients are giants, they lack the perspective of the dwarfs on their shoulders; and although their works are incomparably elegant, it falls to the present to resurrect their dead words. Somewhat like Longinus' image of mimesis as possession, Pierre's image suggests that the legacies of the past rely upon the imitative practices of the present for their survival. There is also a religious undertone to the comment: the Christian era alone can give 'new life' to the pagan relics of the past. Yet the possibility of salvation seems as much a consolation for belatedness as an expression of superiority: the ancients are still giants and the moderns dwarfs.

Renaissance writers made imitation central to their scholarship, theories of education and literary production. The practice of imitation was a means of 'rebirth' (the meaning of the word 'Renaissance'), a way of bringing the illustrious past into the present. It was common for poets in the age to model their careers on that of Virgil, who began by writing pastorals, and only wrote his epic later in life. Classical authors were a constant point of reference and, as we saw in the dissemination of Virgilian epic, a constant source of poetic imagery. Ancient cultures served as models for imitation in other ways as well. For example, in his treatise *The Defence and Illustration of the French Language* (1549), the French poet Joachim Du Bellay argues that modern writers can make their vernacular a mature means of poetic expression only by imitating the Romans. Yet rather than encouraging them to write in Greek or Latin, as it was common to do at the time, Du Bellay called on modern French writers to emulate the ancients in a more fundamental way:

> by what means were they [the Romans] able to enrich their language, even almost to equal that of the Greeks? By imitating the best Greek authors, transforming themselves into them, devouring them; and after they had thoroughly digested them, converted them into blood and nourishment.
>
> (Du Bellay, 2001: 91)

Du Bellay argues that the moderns should follow Roman examples, and he even echoes Seneca's metaphor of imitation as digestion, but there is a clear undertone of hostility in his image. Seneca is never named, and his metaphor of the honey bee is supplanted by the suggestion of a carnivorous beast stalking and attacking its prey. The ancients must be consumed, much as Du Bellay rhetorically 'consumes' Seneca, and much as the Romans themselves consumed the Greeks, to serve as acceptable role models.

Given the cultural divide between the ancient and modern worlds, it is not surprising that medieval and Renaissance writers throughout Europe were deeply self-conscious about, and often highly critical of, the practice of *imitatio*. The period is replete with stories about imitation gone awry. *Don Quixote* (1605), by the Spanish writer Miguel de Cervantes, is probably the best known example of this kind of story.

Cervantes' hero imitates the knights in the chivalric romances he admires, confusing windmills with giants, and labouring for a plain country girl he names Dulcinea. Among the first souls Dante encounters in the *Inferno*, to take another famous instance, are the adulterous lovers Paolo and Francesca, who are caught in a whirlwind that embodies their fatal passion. When Dante questions her, Francesca explains that she and her lover were led into transgression by imitating an Arthurian romance about the adulterous love of Queen Guenevere for Sir Lancelot:

> When we had read how the desired smile
> Was kissed by one who was so true a lover,
> This one, who never shall be parted from me,
> While all his body trembled, kissed my mouth.
> A Gallehault indeed, that book and he
> Who wrote it, too; that day we read no more.
>
> (Dante, 1982: 47)

Francesca attributes her damnation to a reckless act of imitation: Paolo kisses Francesca just as Lancelot kisses Guenevere in the book. The book itself becomes a Gallehault, which is the name of the character who encourages Lancelot and Guenevere in their adultery. To reinforce his criticism of their imitation, Dante places his lovers in the company of two figures from the *Aeneid*, Paris and Helen, whose love was responsible for the Trojan War, and Dido, the queen of Carthage, who committed suicide after Aeneas broke off their affair.

As Thomas Greene has argued, Renaissance *imitatio* led to the first fully historical understanding of the past in Western culture. Renaissance writers experienced the past as profoundly and essentially different from the present. Where Virgil traces a singular line from the mythical fall of Troy to the contemporary Roman Empire, writers of later generations saw the past across an unbridgeable gulf, the so-called Dark Ages of medieval Christianity, during which the great works of antiquity were lost to European culture. Scholars have shown that the Middle Ages were hardly so 'dark' as Renaissance writers suggested, but the myth of recovery provides a good sense of how these writers regarded their own relationship to the past. They were fascinated with the broken physical remains of antiquity: ruins, tombs, fragmentary texts, mutilated statues. These remains appear often in Renaissance art and writing, and mark both the continuing presence of the illustrious past and an abiding sense of loss and belatedness. Imitation became a labour of historical recovery. 'For the ancient writers', Stephen Orgel writes, 'imitation was a process of creation and re-creation, for the Renaissance, it was a process of recovery and preservation as well' (1981: 492). Yet antiquity was only an acceptable role model because it was so removed from the present. The product of an alien culture, Roman works could be appreciated from a critical distance. This distance did not lessen the admiration Renaissance writers felt for antiquity, but it did allow them to reconfirm their own faith alongside their potentially sacrilegious interest in pagan relics. Indeed, as we saw in Pierre's metaphor of the dwarf and the giant, their faith gave these writers an implicit (if ambivalent) sense of superiority over the pagans, whose historical condition excluded them from Christian salvation. Imitating the ancients also meant differentiating oneself from them.

Among the most suggestive Renaissance discussions of *imitatio*, in this regard, is a famous letter by the Italian poet Petrarch describing his ascent of Mount Ventoux, in southern France. The letter, written in 1336, contrasts the imitation of the ancients with the imitation of Christian saints. Petrarch begins by explaining his desire to climb the mountain. Although he states that the only reason for this desire was 'to see its conspicuous height', he resolved to undertake the climb because of something he read:

> It happened while I was reading Roman history again in Livy that I hit upon the passage where Philip, the king of Macedon – the Philip who waged war against the Roman people – 'ascends Mount Haemus in Thessaly, since he believed the rumor that you can see two seas from its top: the Adriatic and the Black Sea'.
>
> (Cassirer *et al.*, 1948: 36)

Petrarch's desire is imitative: he wants to do what the ancient ruler Philip of Macedon did. But this imitation is complicated by ambivalence. Philip was an enemy of Rome, and Livy presents the journey as futile: the king never sees the rumoured view because the summit is shrouded in fog, and he succeeds only in exhausting his troops. Moreover, Mount Haemus was in Thrace, not Thessaly, as Petrarch writes; it was in Thessaly, however, that Philip's armies suffered defeat at the hands of the Romans. The example of Philip suggests that, although the ancients remain a source of inspiration for the present, their path is fatally flawed. Petrarch wants to retain the idea of classical imitation without necessarily endorsing all the ideals of the classical world. Imitation, he implies, is a method, not an end in itself.

This judgement is confirmed by a parallel scene of reading later in the letter. As Petrarch describes his arduous climb, he connects the experience with Christian rather than pagan role models. On his way down from the summit, Petrarch opens a copy of Saint Augustine's autobiographical *Confessions* (398 CE), and is stunned to come upon a passage about the danger of climbing mountains but ignoring one's soul. As Petrarch himself notes, this revelation was also an imitation. Much as he is struck by a passage in Augustine that he comes upon by chance, so Augustine attributes his conversion to a passage in Paul's epistle to the Romans he comes upon by chance. Augustine, in turn, was led to open the Bible by the example of Saint Anthony, who had walked into a church while the Gospel was being read and took the first words he heard as a command. Petrarch moves, in the course of the letter, from the failed imitation of a pagan king to the successful imitation of a Christian saint. This chain of imitations is itself an imitation of a Roman prophetic practice called the *sortes Virgilianae*, in which one opened Virgil's *Aeneid* at random and took the first passage one saw as a prophecy. Augustine and Petrarch in effect 'convert' the *sortes Virgilianae*, and the entire notion of classical imitation, by imitating it as a model for Christian conversion. The imitation of the ancients becomes an *imitatio Christi*, an imitation of Christ.

For much of the period we have been discussing, *imitatio* was the dominant translation and interpretation of mimesis. By the early sixteenth century, the Greek word mimesis had entered the European vernaculars, and scholars began to pay close attention to the texts of Plato and Aristotle, which were finding their way to Europe after surviving for centuries in Arabic translations. Curiously, though, the Greek notion of mimesis that we discussed in the first two chapters did not supplant *imitatio* as a model for understanding poetry in the period.

Indeed, Renaissance literary theory often joined the two ideas. For example, one of the most important works of Renaissance literary theory, Sir Philip Sidney's *Apology for Poetry* (1595), argues that mimesis and *imitatio* work side by side in the best poetry. Sidney highlights poetry's mimetic relationship to nature, as well as its power to foster good imitations in its audience. Mimesis is valuable because it enables *imitatio.* All human arts take nature as their starting point, Sidney argues, but poetry alone has the power to go beyond what nature itself provides. The poet is a second maker who imitates the first creator in the creation of his or her fictions. Following Aristotle's use of organic metaphors, Sidney suggests that the poet 'doth grow in effect another nature', making things better than they are in nature, or creating 'forms such as never were in nature'. 'Nature never set forth the earth in so rich tapestry as divers poets have done', he continues, 'Her world is brazen, the poets only deliver a golden' (Sidney, 2002: 85).

Against Plato, who accuses the poets of lying, and unlike Dante, who depicts Paolo and Francesca as victims of poetic imitation, Sidney argues that the poet 'nothing affirms, and thererfore, never lieth' (Sidney, 2002: 103). Poets are not solely responsible for the veracity of their depictions or the imitative acts of their readers. Indeed, the power of poetry to deliver a golden world is a means of moral teaching. Rather than teaching directly, though, the poet presents exemplary individuals upon whom readers can model themselves. Poets improve upon human nature to correct the all-too-human nature of their readers. To illustrate this Christian ideal for art, Sidney offers a pagan example: the Persian ruler Cyrus as depicted in the Greek philosopher Xenophon's biographical novel *Cyropaedia* (*c.*380 BCE). For Sidney, Xenophon's fictionalized depiction of this ruler, which was also cited by the poet Edmund Spenser as a model for his epic *The Faerie Queene* (1596), is a kind of second nature that provides a better model of virtue than nature itself provides. This depiction, Sidney writes:

> worketh, not only to make a Cyrus, which had been but a particular excellency, as nature might have done, but to bestow a Cyrus upon the world, to make many Cyruses, if they will learn aright why and how that maker made him.
>
> (Sidney, 2002: 85)

As the maker of an ideal Cyrus, Xenophon doubles God's creation: God created Cyrus, but Xenophon recreates him as a pedagogical example. The second creation makes the reasons behind the first creation evident to the reader, and offers Cyrus not just as a historical ruler but as a model for imitation. Following Aristotle, Sidney argues that the power of fiction to offer noble models of conduct makes it the highest form of teaching. Philosophy supplies the precepts of morality, the historian offers examples. Yet philosophy is 'so hard of utterance and so misty to be conceived' that it can only guide those who already understand it. And history is 'so tied, not to what should be but to what is' that its examples are often faulty and cannot reliably deliver generalized lessons. Poetry, however, joins the precept and the example. The poet 'will show you in Tantalus, Atreus, and such like, nothing that is not to be shunned; in Cyrus, Aeneas, Ulysses, each thing to be followed' (Sidney, 2002: 92). Poetic mimesis provides forceful images of virtue and vice, moving the reader to self-improvement.

GENIUS, ORIGINALITY AND THE ANXIETY OF INFLUENCE

The doctrine of *imitatio* comes to an effective, if not actual, end by the close of the eighteenth century, but it was already beginning to lose its hold on European intellectuals a century earlier. One symptom of this change in attitude was the so-called Battle of the Ancients and Moderns, a debate over the authority of classical imitation that occupied thinkers across Europe in the seventeenth and eighteenth centuries. The battle turned upon the relative virtue of ancient and modern culture. Proponents of modernity argued that the moderns had gone beyond their ancient counterparts in scientific method and philosophical insight, and that the doctrine of *imitatio* bound one to outmoded ideals. The French philosopher René Descartes opens his *Discourse on Method* (1637) by detailing his personal rejection of the ancient authorities he studied in school, and his determination 'to search for no knowledge other than what could be found within myself' (1998: 5). Since the power of reason is inherent in the human mind, only fear or habit would make one look to the past for scientific or philosophical authority. Thus Descartes begins his search for a 'first philosophy' alone in a room, and not in the library or the classroom. In order to rebuild philosophy from the foundation, he subjects each of his former beliefs to sceptical doubt. He even refuses to serve as a role model for others:

> But putting forward this essay merely as a story or, if you prefer, as a fable in which, among some examples one can imitate, one will perhaps also find many others which one will have reason not to follow, I hope that it will be useful to some without being harmful to anyone.
>
> (Descartes, 1998: 3)

Descartes' gesture is disingenuous, since he obviously writes to influence his readers, but it clearly demonstrates the decline of *imitatio* as an unquestioned cultural model. The ancients, for Descartes, are a burden rather than a source of inspiration, an outmoded authority rather than a reliable guide. Much the same decline affected the arts in this era. If modern science is an improvement on ancient thought, other critics asked, why should modern artists imitate ancient poets and sculptors?

Needless to say, the doctrine of *imitatio* did not end with the Battle of the Ancients and Moderns, as Pope's continued advocacy for the imitation of ancient writers attests. In fact, the eighteenth century saw the rediscovery of many Greek artefacts and the excavation of the buried Italian city of Pompeii. These archaeological successes led to a renewed interest in the ancient world. The influential German art historian Johann Joachim Winckelmann would argue, in his essay *Thoughts on the Imitation of Greek Works in Painting and Sculpture* (1755), that 'the only way for us to become great, or, if this be possible, inimitable, is to imitate the ancients' (1987: 5). For Winckelmann, imitation is not an end in itself, but a means for modern artists to achieve the heights of the ancients. As ancient artefacts demonstrate, the Greeks saw natural beauty better than the moderns, so modern mimesis should begin, but not end, with *imitatio*: 'If the artist builds upon this groundwork and allows the Greek rules of beauty to guide his hand and mind, he will be on the path which will lead him safely to the imitation of nature' (Winckelmann, 1987: 21). Yet in his *Conjectures on Original Composition*, published only four years after Winckelmann's essay, the British critic and poet Edward Young would deride such imitation as lazy, plagiaristic and opposed to nature. Arguing that the first rule of composition is to 'know thyself', Young suggests that imitation is more likely to stifle the writer's natural genius than to feed it:

> let not great examples, or authorities, browbeat thy reason into too great diffidence of thyself; thyself so reverence, as to prefer the native growth of thy own mind to the richest import from abroad; such borrowed riches make us poor.
>
> (1971: 346)

Young subtly shifts the grounds of the debate, moving nature from the external world to the 'native growth' of the artist's mind. The conventional methods associated with the practice of *imitatio*, he argues, constrain this nature rather than allowing it to grow as it should.

Perhaps the most important account of genius and imitation in the period was that of the German philosopher Immanuel Kant in his 1790 work *The Critique of Judgment*. For Kant, 'genius must be considered the very opposite of a *spirit of imitation*' (1987: 176). Genius, Kant argues, is marked by originality and inspiration and cannot be based on rules and role models. It mimes nature's productive processes, reproduces the laws of nature in a different form, rather than merely reproducing its external forms. The genius does not follow rules, but allows nature to speak directly through his or her work. Where Pope suggests the artist should use the rules that genius provides, Kant argues that works of genius cannot become models for other geniuses to imitate. Works of genius are exemplary, and can inspire other geniuses to create their own works: 'the product of a genius . . . is an example that is meant not to be imitated, but to be followed by another genius' (Kant, 1987: 186–7). Artists who mechanically copy the works of a genius cannot by definition be geniuses themselves. Kant uses the word 'aping' (*Nachäffung*) to describe this bad kind of imitation. Homer can only be an inspiration for another genius, not a guide or source of conventional methods. Mediocre talents might be satisfied with aping conventions, but true genius finds its own rules in the process of creation.

The most advanced theorists of the next generations would follow Young and Kant rather than Pope. Romantic writers of the late eighteenth and early nineteenth centuries overwhelmingly treated genius as a 'native growth', and not a result of 'aping' conventions. This opposition between genius and tradition, creation and imitation, is particularly evident in the marginal annotations that the English poet William Blake wrote in his copy of the *Discourses on Art* (1797), by Sir Joshua Reynolds. Reynolds was the influential first president of the Royal Academy of Art in London, an art school where Blake had been a student, and a strong proponent of *imitatio* in the visual arts. For Reynolds, as for Pope, there is no good art without the imitation of role models. In his sixth discourse, for example, he suggests 'that a painter must not only be of necessity an imitator of the works of nature . . . but he must be as necessarily an imitator of the works of other painters' (Reynolds, 1997: 95). Imitation was a major part of the artistic training of young artists at the Royal Academy, which involved copying plaster casts of ancient statues and of the works of Renaissance masters. But Reynolds maintains that imitation is more than a method of education, and should remain a continuous means of invention even for accomplished artists. The great Italian Renaissance painter Raphael, Reynolds notes, incessantly imitated the ancients as well as his older contemporaries. Indeed, 'it was from his having taken so many models, that he became a model for all succeeding painters; always imitating, and always original' (Reynolds, 1997: 104). For Reynolds, genius is 'the child of imitation'; the genius does not break the rules of art or, as Kant asserts, produce entirely new rules, but applies fixed and accepted principles in new ways (1997: 96).

For Blake, by contrast, genius can only be born, not taught, and is embodied in the mind and works of unique individuals, not in traditions or conventions. 'Genius dies with its Possessor & comes not again till Another is Born with it', he writes in one annotation to the sixth discourse (Reynolds, 1997: 310). In another annotation, he suggests that imitation, far from being a means of better grasping nature, goes wholly against nature:

> How ridiculous it would be to see the Sheep Endeavouring to walk like the Dog, or the Ox striving to trot like the Horse; just as Ridiculous is it to see One man Striving to Imitate Another. Man varies from Man more than Animal from Animal of different species.
>
> (Reynolds, 1997: 309)

For Blake, artists do not learn by imitating other artists, but must develop according to their own nature. One genius is to another as a sheep is to a dog: wholly different species with distinct natures and abilities. In an annotation to Reynolds' first discourse, Blake makes this claim explicit:

> I do not believe that Rafael taught Mich. Angelo or that Mich. Ang. taught Rafael, any more than I believe that the Rose teaches the Lilly how to grow or the Apple tree teaches the Pear tree how to bear fruit.
> (Reynolds, 1997: 292)

Genius develops like a flower, producing beauty according to its inherent nature, not according to the model provided by another genius.

The decline of *imitatio* at the end of the eighteenth century ushered in a literary and artistic world that would strike writers such as Virgil, Erasmus and even Pope as very strange. It is surely no coincidence, for example, that the same period in which Young and Blake were writing saw the development of the first copyright laws. Such laws define artistic products as a possession of the individual and his or her descendants, and not as the common property of humanity. Only the author and his or her designated agents can legitimately profit from this 'intellectual property'. Copyright redefines *imitatio* as a form of plagiarism or intellectual piracy. Imitating the work of another artist is akin to stealing his or her most personal possession. The decline of *imitatio* and the rise of the ideal of genius also produce what the literary critic Harold Bloom has called the 'anxiety of influence'. This term describes the way that Romantic and post-Romantic poets inevitably engage in an imaginative struggle with the prior writers who have influenced them. No longer a partnership with the 'giants' of the past, or even a rivalry between pagan masters and Christian disciples, artistic creation is a life-and-death struggle with a predecessor who threatens to overwhelm the poet's voice and whose influence must therefore be repressed, deflected or transformed. 'A poem', Bloom writes, 'is a poet's melancholy at his lack of priority' (1973: 96). Where genius and originality define artistic value, the past can only be perceived as a threat, and the practice of *imitatio* as proof of weakness.

Although, as I have suggested, imitation remains an important part of both high and popular culture today, no less important in many ways than it was for Roman or Renaissance writers, it has never regained the public status it once held, and is often condemned or equated with theft. Artistic production seems to us, as it did to Blake, the unique expression of an individual, and originality is the new coin of the realm. Tradition and convention are shackles to be broken, or authorities against which one is almost expected to rebel. The coincident rise of copyright laws and the anxiety of influence in the eighteenth century marks the passing of *imitatio* as a model for literary production, and its eclipse as the predominant Western idea of mimesis.

4

THEATRE AND THEATRICALITY

SPECTACLE AND SPECTATOR

In his *Confessions*, Saint Augustine (354–430 CE) tells the story of a student, Alypius, who was taken to a Roman gladiatorial contest by some acquaintances. Alypius is morally opposed to such spectacles, but agrees to go along, confident in his ability to resist temptation. Although he covers his eyes at first, the sound of the crowd cheering a gladiator's death rouses his curiosity. When he opens his eyes to look, he is fatally drawn in by the spectacle:

> The din had pierced his ears and forced him to open his eyes, laying his soul open to receive the wound which struck it down. . . . When he saw the blood, it was as though he had drunk a deep draught of savage passion. Instead of turning away, he fixed his eyes upon the scene and drank in all its frenzy, unaware of what he was doing. He was no longer a man who had come to the arena, but simply one of the crowd he had joined.
>
> (Augustine, 1961: 122)

The spectacle Alypius watches is not mimetic, but Augustine's account closely follows Plato's critique of tragedy. Much like Plato, Augustine associates theatre with violence and irrational emotions, with the victory of 'savage passion' over reason and orderly thought. Augustine stresses in particular the sensory force of the show. Alypius is roused to curiosity by the roar of the crowd, and is gripped, against all his moral beliefs, by the sight of blood. There is, it would seem, something dangerous about spectacle as such. Alypius goes into the arena a moral man, but leaves it fallen.

Augustine's story belongs to a long tradition in Western thought that Jonas Barish has called the 'antitheatrical prejudice'. From Plato to current critics of sex and violence in the popular media, the theatre and other performance genres have been subjected to more abuse and official censorship than any other art form. The antitheatrical prejudice entails much more than the criticism of certain plays, though, encompassing what Barish calls an 'ontological malaise', a thoroughgoing fear of the theatrical in all aspects of life (Barish, 1981: 2). This malaise has left its mark on everyday language. As Barish notes, almost every common metaphor about theatre is negative. We praise the 'poetic' or the 'picturesque', but distrust the 'staged' or the 'histrionic' (Barish, 1981: 1). Theatre also traditionally bears the taint of immorality. Throughout Western history, actors and actresses have been regarded as potential seducers or the moral equivalent of prostitutes. The current tabloid obsession with the love lives of movie stars follows from this ancient link between performers and sexuality. Questions about the morality of performers, notes Mendel Kohansky (1984), have relegated actors and actresses to the social margins in almost every world culture. This marginality can render them pariahs or, as in modern Western media culture, objects of extreme fascination. Whether revered or reviled, though, actors and actresses seem a breed apart, somehow transfigured by their connection to stage or screen.

The imagery and associations of the theatre comprise another of the central thematic elements of the theory of mimesis. Theatre is not, strictly speaking, identical with mimesis. But theatre and theatricality have been so central to the theory since antiquity that it is nearly impossible to separate the two ideas. While the fortunes of *imitatio* rose and fell over time, theatre has rarely been regarded favourably. Plato and

Aristotle, for example, both seek to minimize, even dispense with, the most theatrical elements of tragedy. Plato simply banished the tragic poets, while allowing those poets and performers who do not 'disguise' themselves to remain. Stories have a useful social function, he implies, but theatricality is problematic. Aristotle's banishment is more subtle but no less comprehensive. As Samuel Weber has noted, Aristotle defines spectacle as a mere medium, a means of presenting the plot, and not a source of independent effects (2004: 100). Spectacle is the least artistic element of tragedy, Aristotle argues, and does not contribute to the true tragic effect, which, as we have seen, is produced by the plot: 'For the power of tragedy . . . is felt even apart from representation and actors' (1951: 64). Aristotle 'saves' mimesis from Plato by taking it out of the theatre.

Why does theatre rouse such anxiety? Why is it regarded as at once dangerous and dispensable? Augustine offers a clue. Despite his weakness for spectacles, Alypius was endowed with 'much natural disposition to goodness' (Augustine, 1961: 120). Had he seen a man wounded in the street, he would surely have responded with pity rather than 'savage passion'. Violence in the street is not materially different from violence in the gladiatorial arena. What distinguishes them is the form of theatre itself, which, Augustine suggests, distances us from others and renders the morally repugnant irresistibly attractive. Augustine knows this from experience for he, too, was once addicted to theatre. Instead of seeking happiness and avoiding sorrow, he notes in his account of this addiction, we are happy in the theatre only when we and others suffer: 'The audience is not called upon to offer help but only to feel sorrow, and the more they are pained the more they applaud the author' (Augustine, 1961: 56). Spectacles transform the emotions, making pain a source of pleasure and rendering ethical feelings a matter of aesthetic enjoyment. Although he objects to certain kinds of shows, then, what most troubles Augustine about the theatre is the structural relationship of spectator to spectacle. Alypius falls not just because of what he sees, but because of the way, and the position from which, he sees it.

Although they do not share his antitheatricality, many recent theorists implicitly follow Augustine in defining theatrical mimesis in terms of the interaction of spectator and spectacle. *Imitatio,* I noted in the last chapter, reconceived of the distinction between copy and original as a relationship between model and imitator, idealized past and belated present. Theatrical metaphors, by contrast, figure mimesis as a representation *for* someone, and not only a representation *of* something else. They highlight what theorists have called the 'performative' quality of mimesis, its explicit address to or dependence upon an audience. This quality is arguably inherent in all forms of artistic mimesis, but it is particularly true of the theatre. Theatre is incomplete, almost unimaginable, without an audience. 'Theater comes into existence', writes the performance theorist Richard Schechner, 'when a separation occurs between spectators and performers' (2003: 137). The conceptual division between actor and audience characterizes all kinds of performances, from Broadway shows to classroom lectures, sporting events, wedding ceremonies and political demonstrations.

Theatrical mimesis, in this regard, arises not from the distinction between a real original and an illusory copy but from a particular kind of action and attention, from the 'doings' of actor and audience rather than the 'being' of the spectacle. Despite the 'material tangibility of its means', literary critic Jan Mukarovsky has argued, mimesis in the theatre 'pervades the entire auditorium' (1978: 203). The theatre theorist Josette Féral has pushed this idea even further, suggesting that theatrical mimesis is the result of a 'perceptual dynamics' of seeing and being seen (2002: 105). Theatre opens up a 'cleft in quotidian space', dividing the spatial and temporal 'inside' of the performance from its everyday 'outside', and setting certain places and actions apart from the flow of everyday life (Féral, 2002: 97). Féral offers the example of so-called 'invisible theatre', in which actors stage conflicts in public spaces without letting the 'audience' in on the plot. If the actors eventually signal the theatrical context of their conflict, the space is immediately transformed from quotidian to theatrical. The perceptual dynamics of theatre can turn a subway car into a temporary stage, and make any pedestrian into an unwitting performer or audience.

To this extent, theatrical mimesis is engendered and sustained largely by social conventions. Whereas *imitatio* is based on the conscious use of conventions, though, we rarely reflect upon common theatrical conventions. Let us take, for example, the so-called 'fourth wall' that is said to divide the stage from the auditorium. In modern theatrical performances, the actors typically pretend they are speaking only to each other, and the audience remains silent throughout the performance, as if it were looking through an invisible wall. These conventions draw an imaginary line between reality and appearance, the quotidian original and the theatrical copy. But this line exists only in the beliefs and practices of the participants. In fact, the fourth wall is a recent development in theatre history. Audiences in ancient Greece, for example, hardly sat in rapt silence. Tragedies were performed during daylight in an enormous and often noisy amphitheatre. Elizabethan theatre audiences entirely surrounded the stage, which was largely devoid of scenery or props. In seventeenth-century France, it was common for members of the audience to sit on the stage, converse with actors during the performance, and request that they perform scenes more than once. There was little sense in any of these contexts that the stage was a separate world, or that the actors represented real people. Modern conventions, as Anne-Britt Gran has noted, only solidified in the 1850s; it was not until the 1880s that it became common to dim the house lights during the performance (Gran, 2002: 259–60). The idea of the fourth wall makes the stage into a mimetic copy of the world, but this copy is as much the collective illusion of the actors and the audience as it is a quality of the spectacle itself.

THEATRUM MUNDI

Because it depends so heavily on social conventions, theatrical mimesis underscores the limits of Plato's foundational distinction between copy and original. For all of their attention to the effects of art on the audience, Plato and Aristotle both regard mimesis as a thing with definable qualities, even if its chief property is a lack of unique properties. They restrict their definition to concrete artworks that are perceptible to the senses, and compare or contrast it to physical objects such as mirrors, couches and animals. But none of the material things that contribute to theatrical mimesis – stage, backdrop, props, actors, audience, texts – is inherently mimetic. They only become so in and through a given production and by virtue of the conventional beliefs and practices of the participants on stage and in the audience. Theatrical mimesis, to this extent, is at once nowhere and everywhere. It is a form of attention, a conceptual envelope that surrounds and transfigures people and things rather than a discrete object, location or form of action. The words theatre and theory, we might note, share the same Greek root: *thea*, meaning to 'look' or 'view'. Theory, like theatre, assumes the possibility of finding an external standpoint, of distinguishing the knowing subject from the known object.

To this extent, there is no reason why theatrical mimesis should be restricted to formal theatre, or even to typically theatrical behaviour or situations. Given the right perceptual dynamic, as Féral has suggested, theatrical mimesis can 'happen' anywhere or anytime. In fact, this notion underlies one of the oldest and most influential Western metaphors for life: the *theatrum mundi* or theatre of the world. This metaphor imagines life as a play, with the world a stage, each person an actor, and God the all-seeing audience. In effect, it theatricalizes the world, turning all of life into a mimetic spectacle. *Theatrum mundi* metaphors have been common since antiquity, but William Shakespeare offers the most familiar version of it in *As You Like It*:

> All the world's a stage,
> And all the men and women merely players;
> They have their exits and their entrances,
> And one man in his time plays many parts,
> His acts being seven ages.
>
> (1974: 381/II, vii, 139–43)

As Lynda G. Christian demonstrates in her study of this metaphor (1987), the *theatrum mundi* embodies many different philosophical and theological attitudes. For some, it defines life as a tragedy or a comedy, as deeply serious or frivolous and false. For others, it depicts human action as scripted, directed by a higher power (God or fate). In some contexts it figures the spectator as a stoically detached observer of life, and in others as a helpless victim of a tragic spectacle that unravels before him or her. For the melancholic Jaques, the speaker of Shakespeare's lines, the image points to the vanity of human life. We each play a series of parts – infant, student, lover, soldier, and so forth – which circumscribe our actions and choices. There is no real progression from birth to old age, only a change of costumes, and every life follows the same plot.

For other Renaissance thinkers, however, the image of the theatre offered a vision of human freedom. In his *Oration on the Dignity of Man* (1486), the Italian humanist Pico della Mirandola defines human beings as at once actors and spectators of creation. They alone are able to 'observe whatever is in the world' and become 'maker and molder' of themselves (Cassirer *et al.*, 1948: 225). Although both the theatre and the performer are made by another, humans have the ability to improvise their roles freely. Pico's statement is a foundational instance of what the literary scholar Stephen Greenblatt (1980) has called Renaissance self-fashioning. This term highlights the ways in which individuals during the period conceived of social life as a form of role playing, of presenting a carefully crafted self to an audience of peers and the powerful. Both Jaques and Pico regard life as a form of theatrical mimesis. But while Jaques sees human actions as a series of copies, in which we mime roles given by nature or custom, Pico suggests that we can stand outside our various roles, control our performance and even choose new parts to play.

We find a powerful version of the *theatrum mundi* metaphor in the Italian political theorist Niccolò Machiavelli's widely influential treatise *The Prince* (1513). Machiavelli departs radically from classical and Christian traditions of political theory in arguing for the separation of ethics and politics. Political stability, he argues, often demands that the ruler act unethically, but it is essential that the prince fashion himself as an ethical ruler to ensure the love and respect of his or her subjects. Thus the prince must be 'a great feigner and dissimulator' (Machiavelli, 1995: 97), in other words, a skilled performer and role player. Indeed, actually being ethical can be dangerous, for the prince might be forced by deeply held moral principles into politically inexpedient choices. Machiavelli turns Plato's account of mimesis on its head: the fact that it is possible to appear good without actually being good is, for the ambitious ruler, of great political value. Machiavelli also argues that the prince should be a skilled director. He refers with admiration to the legendary Duke Valentino, Cesare Borgia, who often staged political 'spectacles' to preserve his rule. In one example Machiavelli narrates, Borgia has a widely hated minister executed, and displays his decapitated body in the public square. '[T]his spectacle', Machiavelli writes, 'satisfied and intimidated the people at the same time' (1995: 61). The mere execution of the minister might have been a popular act, but it would not have had the same politically useful effect as a theatrical production. If life is like a theatre, Machiavelli implies, the prince must recognize and exploit the fact that he is on stage, and not a passive member of the audience.

Renaissance artists and philosophers were fascinated by the powerful and disturbing implications of the theatrical metaphors in writers such as Pico and Machiavelli. There is, perhaps, no better staging of these implications than Shakespeare's *Hamlet* (*c.*1599). The literary critic Robert Weimann argues that this play is Shakespeare's 'most sustained theoretical statement' on the subject of mimesis (1985: 279). *Hamlet* is rife with doubles, repetitions and references to the traditional language and imagery of mimesis. But perhaps the most pervasive mimetic theme in the play is theatre itself. *Hamlet* can be read as a meditation on the *theatrum mundi* metaphor, and in particular on its suggestion that the boundaries dividing theatre and everyday life, acting and politics are unstable. Nearly all of the characters in the play try their hand at acting, directing or writing formal or 'invisible' performances, and all of the major characters play the role of audience members. Shakespeare suggests that theatrical paradigms are at once inevitable and deeply problematic. The characters rely on theatrical techniques to elicit truths about life, but theatrical mimesis in this play has only three results: death, political disorder and more mimesis.

Perhaps the most famous piece of acting in the play is Hamlet's decision to 'put an antic disposition on', and persuade the court that he has gone mad (Shakespeare, 1974: 1151/I, v, 172). Hamlet plays this role to reveal (or confirm) a truth. He has been told by the ghost of his slain father, the former king of Denmark, that he was murdered by the new king, Hamlet's uncle and stepfather Claudius. Hamlet imagines his new role as a means of confirming the ghost's accusation, of showing that Claudius is only feigning honesty and justice. The appearance of madness, he believes, will give him cover from suspicion, and produce evidence of his uncle's guilt. In short, he plays both actor and covert audience to unmask what he sees as his uncle's theatricality, his imitation of a legitimate king. Theatre, for Hamlet, is a tool of theory, a mimetic means of observing mimesis. But it is perhaps ominous that the revelation of truth should arise from the performance of madness.

Indeed, Hamlet's performance only produces more theatricality, as members of the court mirror the prince in using theatrical techniques for their own ends. Polonius is the most significant mirror for Hamlet in this regard. At the beginning of act three, for example, he stages an 'invisible' theatrical performance, ironically to discern the cause of Hamlet's madness. He directs his daughter Ophelia to read a book as Hamlet approaches, and then hides with the King and Queen, 'seeing, unseen', to observe what happens (Shakespeare, 1974: 1160/III, i, 32). Each spectator, however, comes away with a very different interpretation of the performance. Ophelia feels pity for Hamlet, and casts him as a tragic hero: 'O, woe is me, / T' have seen what I have seen!' (Shakespeare, 1974: 1161/III, i, 160–1). The King, by contrast, regards Hamlet's performance as deceptive. His behaviour, he suggests, 'was not like madness', and reveals that Hamlet is plotting against him (Shakespeare, 1974: 1161/III, i, 164). Polonius, finally, is persuaded that Hamlet's madness arises from unrequited love for Ophelia. The fact that the audience at this impromptu play cannot agree on a lesson is suggestive. Like Hamlet, Polonius looks for truth and a course of action in theatre, but finds only the prior assumptions that each member of the audience has brought to the show. Polonius again resorts to theatrical techniques at the end of act three when he watches a scene between Hamlet and his mother from behind some curtains in the room. When Gertrude cries out for help, Polonius stirs, and Hamlet thrusts his sword through the curtain, killing his secreted audience. Although theatre is based on a distinction between actors and audience, the death of Polonius indicates that the lines between spectacle and spectators are always, and dangerously, in flux.

All of the problems of theatre in *Hamlet* are epitomized in a play-within-the-play in act three. Hamlet here takes on the role of director, and makes himself the spectator of his uncle's response as a member of the audience. A group of actors has come to Elsinore, and Hamlet asks them to stage a play called *The Murder of Gonzago,* which imitates the ghost's account of his murder by Claudius. Like Polonius, Hamlet here imagines that theatre can reveal truth. This truth, however, concerns the moral status of the audience, not the subject of the drama:

I have heard
That guilty creatures sitting at a play
Have by the very cunning of the scene
Been strook so to the soul that presently
They have proclaim'd their malefactions.
(Shakespeare, 1974: 1159/II, ii, 588–92)

A public confrontation with Claudius would make the King an actor. But with the King a member of the audience, Hamlet believes, the King's catharsis and confession will coincide. Hamlet gives voice to this belief in his instructions to the actors before the performance. The purpose of acting, he tells them, 'is to hold as 'twere the mirror up to nature, to show virtue her feature, scorn her own image, and the very age and body of the time his form and pressure' (Shakespeare, 1974: 1161–2/III, ii, 22–4). Where Plato condemns the mirror of mimesis for its mere reproduction of physical nature, Hamlet sees the actor's mimesis, like his own performance of madness, as a means of revealing the hidden truths of human nature. Acting is at once mimetic and a way of unmasking what the audience dissimulates.

True to its effects throughout the play, Hamlet's theatricality fails to produce an unequivocal truth. Following the performance of *The Murder of Gonzago*, Claudius becomes suspicious of Hamlet. In effect, the play has revealed as much about its would-be director as about its audience. Claudius thus conspires to direct his own 'bad performance' (Shakespeare, 1974: 1177/IV, vii, 151), in which Laertes, Ophelia's brother, engages the unwitting Hamlet in a fencing match with a poisoned rapier. The end of this performance is bloody for both its actors and the audience. All the major figures in the play lie dead, and Fortinbras, the prince of Norway, is poised to take political control of Denmark. At the brink of death, Hamlet asks his friend Horatio to tell the truth about this scene: 'Horatio, I am dead; / Thou livest. Report me and my cause aright / To the unsatisfied' (Shakespeare, 1974: 1185/V, ii, 138–9). Horatio ironically fulfils Hamlet's wish, though, by staging yet another play:

give order that these bodies
High on a stage be placed to the view,

And let me speak to th' yet unknowing world
How these things came about.

(Shakespeare, 1974: 1185/V, ii, 377–80)

Horatio relies upon theatrical techniques to tell the truth about Hamlet's death. He claims that this story will prevent 'more mischance / Of plots and errors' among those who hear it, but Shakespeare implies that Horatio has fallen into the same error that fells Hamlet, Polonius and Claudius (Shakespeare, 1974: 1185/V, ii, 394). If all the world is a stage, then there is no end to the performance, at least for the living and maybe even for the dead.

ACTING, NATURALLY

Hamlet plays out many implications of the *theatrum mundi* metaphor. For Shakespeare, we might suggest, all knowing and worldly action is inherently theatrical. But this is not always a good thing. Renaissance writers such as Shakespeare, of course, would have understood the idea theologically: worldly existence is a vain show, and we are all actors for God, who ultimately judges our performance. But *Hamlet* also raises powerful questions about the nature of acting, emotion and social interaction. When the actors arrive at Elsinore, for example, Hamlet asks one of them to recite a speech. He is particularly impressed with the actor's rendering of grief:

Is it not monstrous that this player here,
But in a fiction, in a dream of passion,
Could force his soul so to his own conceit
That from her working all his visage wanned,
Tears in his eyes, distraction in his aspect,
A broken voice, and his whole function suiting
With forms to his conceit? And all for nothing!

(Shakespeare, 1974: 1159/II, ii, 551–7)

Although we all might be said to play roles in everyday life (we shall return to this idea shortly), professional actors possess the unique ability to feign emotions they do not feel. Hamlet marvels at the way the actor can change his external features to match an apparent internal emotion. The actor produces signs of emotion – white face, tears, broken voice – by 'forcing' his soul, not by actually feeling emotions appropriate to such signs. He produces the appearance of feelings that are not true, and feels for people who do not exist.

The actor's 'monstrous' ability to mime emotion was central to eighteenth-century thought. As scholars such as Michael Fried (1980) and David Marshall (1986) have demonstrated, the imagery of acting and theatre are pervasive in the art, literature and moral theory of the period. Acting offers a resonant metaphor for the relationship between art and the beholder, and between the private self and its public roles. Theatre also comes to epitomize the hypocrisy of social life, the conviction that the private self is truer and more natural than its conventionalized public performance for others. Gebauer and Wulf argue that the interest in acting in the eighteenth century reflects a thoroughgoing 'internalization' of mimesis. The division between copy and original that defined mimesis in Plato, they suggest, comes to characterize the division between mind and body, emotion and expression. In addition to being a mirror held up to physical nature, mimesis is a mirror of the inner self (Gebauer and Wulf, 1995: 157).

But this rethinking of mimesis presents new problems. Unlike most other mimetic artists, the actor is physically present to the audience. The actor's body is part of the work, an essential means of creating mimetic illusions. Since the 'original' of an emotion is unknowable to anyone other than the person who feels it, however, this presence is potentially deceptive. The mimed emotion of a skilled actor is all but impossible to distinguish from genuine emotion. In neither case can we reliably compare the external copy to its internal original, the mirrored emotion to the truth it reflects. One is thus forced to ask whether the actor is exemplary or exceptional, whether, that is, all human beings are actors or actors are somehow monstrous. In his novel *Wilhelm Meister's Apprenticeship* (1796), Johann Wolfgang von Goethe depicts his titular protagonist as a middle-class Everyman who moves from the stage (where he plays Hamlet) to respectable society. Somewhat like Pico, Goethe uses acting as a metaphor for self-creation, and in particular for the new bourgeois social mobility available in eighteenth-century European society. For other writers, however, acting is a near-synonym for hypocrisy and deceptiveness. In Jane Austen's novel *Mansfield Park* (1814), for example, the amoral Henry Crawford persuades a group of reluctant but impressionable young people to stage a theatrical production while the master of the house is away. His enthusiasm for acting points to the shallow and changeable nature Henry will display throughout the book.

Jean-Jacques Rousseau provides the most striking and influential expression of the view of acting we later find in Austen and many other writers of the period. The actor's gift, Rousseau writes, in the *Letter to D'Alembert on the Theater* (1758):

> is the art of counterfeiting himself, of putting on another character than his own, of appearing different than he is, of becoming passionate in cold blood, of saying what he does not think as naturally as if he really did think it, and finally, of forgetting his own place by dint of taking another's.
>
> (Rousseau, 1960: 79)

Rousseau sees an obvious danger in this gift. The actor, he notes, is skilled in deception and has 'become adept in habits which can be innocent only in the theater' (Rousseau, 1960: 80). Let loose in the city, the professional deceiver can become a Machiavellian political actor, or a seducer of the young. This threat is heightened by the internal distance the actor must cultivate from his or her natural emotions. What the actor displays on stage is a pale imitation of true feeling. And much as the theatre audience, according to Rousseau, believes it has 'satisfied all the rights of humanity' when it feels pity for a fictional character, so actors sacrifice their humanity by giving themselves over to the roles they play and the emotions they mime (1960: 25). The actor is 'fit for all sorts of roles except for the most noble of all, that of man, which he abandons' (Rousseau, 1960: 80).

One of the most suggestive responses to this account of acting came from Rousseau's contemporary, the French philosopher Denis Diderot. Diderot's dialogue, 'The Paradox of the Actor', written around 1770 but not published until 1830, defends the actor against Rousseau's attack, and in so doing subversively questions the belief that there is a meaningful difference in society between real and mimed emotion. For Diderot, the actor is not an aberration. Rather, actors epitomize an uncomfortable truth about all emotional expression. Actors, he argues, are great imitators of emotion, who observe and classify the conventional signs of human emotion, and then train themselves, though a laborious process of rehearsal and self-observation, to mirror these signs for the audience. The actor's talent, he writes, 'consists not in feeling . . . but in giving such a scrupulous rendering of the outward signs of feeling that you're taken in' (Diderot, 1994: 107). In fact, real feelings interfere with this mimetic process. The best actors 'are too busy watching, identifying and imitating to be deeply affected within themselves' (Diderot, 1994: 106). As opposed to the theory of 'method acting' associated with such modern teachers as Konstantin Stanislavsky and Lee Strasberg, in which actors are encouraged to 'live' the characters they play, Diderot argues that actors should have 'no feeling', and should not identify with their character. They need only the 'power to imitate anything' (Diderot, 1994: 103). Theatrical emotions do not mirror the actor's true feelings, but produce the appearance of feeling for the audience.

Actors are notable for their skill in miming emotion, Diderot goes on to suggest, but they are not unique. Indeed, the actor's ability to distinguish genuine from performed feeling is necessary for many social roles, where real emotions might hinder the 'performer'. 'At the least unexpected thing', Diderot writes, 'the man of feeling loses his head: he will never be a great king, a great minister, a great general, a great advocate or a great doctor' (1994: 106). Those driven by feeling alone lack any internal distance from their emotions, and cannot control the way they present themselves to others. Diderot notes that there are crucial differences between stage and society. Just as a person caught up in real emotional turmoil would look ridiculous on the stage, so the actor's exaggerated stage gestures would look false and contrived at a social function. Rather, the key to both acting and social interaction is the ability to adapt one's performance to a given audience, to match the spectacle to the spectators. In the 'great comedy of the world', Diderot explains, 'all the hot-blooded people are on the stage; all the men of genius are in the pit' (1994: 106). The great actor subtly reverses the relationship between actor and audience, using the unwitting show of emotions by others to refine his or her performance. But the actor also epitomizes a more fundamental truth about emotion and society.

As Diderot notes, it is only by external signs that we can recognize any emotion: 'it's impossible to appreciate what goes on inside us in any other way' (1994: 140). A real emotion and an effectively mimed emotion look exactly the same to the spectator. Where Rousseau complains that actors copy real emotions, Diderot suggests that real emotions are always akin to a copy for their audience. We are all on stage, but only some of us realize we are performing.

The relationship between acting and society that figures so prominently in the works of eighteenth-century writers would gain an important new resonance in the twentieth century. If society is like a theatre, it is suggested, then change in theatre might produce change in the social world as well. 'I am not one of those who believe that civilization has to change in order for the theater to change', writes Antonin Artaud, in his treatise *Theater and Its Double* (1938), 'but I do believe that the theater, utilized in the highest and most difficult sense possible, has the power to influence the aspect and formation of things' (1958: 79). For Artaud, this means breaking down the line between spectacle and spectator, and giving theatre the immediacy and force of train wrecks, earthquakes and plagues. For the German playwright Bertolt Brecht, Artaud's near-contemporary, it also meant radically transforming the craft of the actor. Brecht was highly critical of what he called the Aristotelian model of theatre, based, as he saw it, on tightly knit plots and emotional identification with the characters. Placed into a kind of aesthetic trance, the audience for Aristotelian theatre loses itself in the plot, and leaves the theatre pleasurably drained. For the Marxist Brecht, catharsis is beneficial only for the status quo, as it renders the audience passive and uncritical.

In place of this passive attitude, Brecht argues for the cultivation of the 'alienation effect'. The alienation effect seeks to break the illusion of the fourth wall, making the audience aware of its identifications and its presence in the theatre. Brecht proposed a variety of techniques to cultivate this effect, such as leaving the house lights on during the performance. The most important techniques, however, pertain to acting. Actors, he argued, should avoid 'living' their role. Instead, they should act as if the performance were a commentary in the third person: 'The actor does not allow himself to be completely transformed into the character he is portraying. He is not Lear, Harpagon, Schweik; he shows them' (Brecht, 1964: 137). Brecht encourages his actors to address the audience directly, to read stage directions aloud, and to be critical of the character's actions. The key performance technique in epic theatre is what Brecht calls the 'gest'. A gest is a stylized motion, expression or tone of voice that summarizes and reveals the world view of a given character. Through its repetition in the play, the gest comes to embody the 'social relationships prevailing between people of a given period' (Brecht, 1964: 139). An often-cited example of the gest comes from a production of Brecht's play *Mother Courage* (1939). The title character in the play is a lower-middle-class businesswoman, whose family is destroyed by a war that she supports because it is good for business. After each economic transaction, the actress playing this part would snap her purse shut with a loud click. The gesture comes to define the character, but also summarizes her willingness to put profit before people.

In a broader sense, all the techniques of epic theatre 'alienate' the conventions of acting and performance. Where Diderot suggests actors should manipulate the conventions of emotional expression to produce mimetic effects, Brecht suggests they should unmask stage conventions to undermine mimesis. Brecht tellingly compares epic actors, in this regard, to circus clowns. Whereas a traditional Western actor might express sadness by inducing real tears, a clown will make exaggerated gestures, such as rubbing his or her eyes, or drawing tears onto her face with make-up (Brecht, 1964: 91). Rather than 'living' the emotion, clowns ostentatiously 'perform' it with conventional gestures. The ultimate aim of the alienation effect, Brecht argues, is to 'historicize' the events of the play. Rather than seeing situations or character types as natural and unalterable, Brecht wants to encourage the audience to treat the present day 'with the same detachment as the historian adopts with regard to' the past, or that the actor adopts with regard to his or her role (1964: 140). Alienating artistic conventions becomes a means of unveiling the coercive effects of social conventions. Rather than being purged and pacified by the work, the audience should be left 'productively disposed even after the spectacle is over', aware of the power of theatrical conventions (Brecht, 1964: 205). Even more, they should learn to apply what they have learned about theatrical conventions to life beyond the stage, recognizing that artistic and social conventions alike are products of human choices and human history, and thus open to criticism and change.

'THE NEVER ENDING SHOW'

Brecht's theory of acting was highly influential in its own right, but it was also part of a larger interest in theatrical metaphors among twentieth-century artists and intellectuals. We shall explore the theoretical context of this notion, including the important idea that identity is 'performative', in chapter 6. But many of the insights that inform current theories of identity underlie accounts of theatre from Augustine to Brecht. Because it is produced by conventional beliefs and practices, theatrical mimesis always has social and political implications. Augustine's Christian antitheatricality and Brecht's Marxist theatricality alike see theatre as a matter of world-historical importance. Both writers implicitly suggest that theatre has the power to change the world for better or worse. For most of the theorists we have discussed in this chapter, though, the relationship between theatre and social life is instrumental or figurative. Theatre is a tool for affecting the world, or a metaphor for worldly existence. For an important line of social and cultural theorists in the twentieth century, however, the *theatrum mundi* is much more than a metaphor. All of these writers regard theatricality and the relationship between actor and audience as a fundamental and inescapable aspect of human life, and not just a secondary or artificial elaboration on an otherwise non-theatrical reality.

One of the earliest and most suggestive arguments for the fundamental theatricality of life comes in the Russian director Nicolas Evreinoff's book *The Theater in Life* (1922). Evreinoff identifies an instinctual 'will to theatricality' that underlies the formal traditions and institutions of the theatre. This will is not limited to humans. When a cat toys with a mouse, or a plant mimics its surroundings, each assumes a role, wears a mask. The cat plays at indifference until the mouse attempts to escape. And the plant performs 'a motionless, prudent pantomime' to conceal itself. This 'highly artistic masquerade', Evreinoff writes:

> infinitely rich in devices and in wardrobe, goes on around us in a never ending procession. Is this not theater? Do not the little silent actors obey in their everyday behaviour the purely theatrical principle of 'pretending to be different from that which one really is'?
>
> (1970: 12–13)

This theatrical principle governs all manner of human behaviour as well, from children's play to table manners, grooming routines, even education, which trains us for a social role. Every time we approach a mirror, pose for a photograph or daydream, Evreinoff notes, we play actor and spectator at once: 'you mimic the appearance of greatness, attractiveness, imposing earnestness, decision' (1970: 51). In each case, the unwitting actor seeks to transform what nature has given, to change his or her appearance, to become someone or something else. 'The main thing for us', he writes, 'is *not to be ourselves*. This is the theatrical imperative of our souls' (Evreinoff, 1970: 65). Evreinoff pushes to its limits Aristotle's claim that imitation is natural: theatre is not a means to other ends (pleasure, learning) but an inherent biological drive towards transformation and differentiation. All life, Evreinoff states in a chapter title, is a 'never ending show'.

Although theatricality is a natural instinct, its effects are highly conventional. Rather than being opposed or distinct, the natural and the theatrical are part of a continuum. Both arise out of the relationship between actor and audience:

> There exists at the moment of theatrical perception a sort of silent agreement, a sort of *tacitus consensus*, between the spectator and the player whereby the former undertakes to assume a certain attitude, and not other, toward the 'make believe' of acting, while the latter undertakes to live up to this assumed attitude as best he can.
>
> (Evreinoff, 1970: 141)

The most challenging role, for Evreinoff, is naturalness itself, since it demands the unquestioning participation of both parties: the actor earnestly performs familiar conventions, and the audience agrees not to recognize their conventionality. The effort to repress theatricality, to act naturally, only makes one a bad actor. This is true both in theatre and in society. There is, Evreinoff suggests, an invisible 'stage manager' who directs the course of public life and ensures its smooth operation. Each culture and each epoch has its own 'theatrical characteristics': wardrobe, scenery and a 'script' governing manners in public (Evreinoff, 1970: 100). Openly rejecting these conventions does not get one closer to nature. Rather, it replaces one set of theatrical conventions with another.

Rousseau's fulminations against the falsity of acting and society, for example, 'simply lent a new shade to the old styles and harmonies of life' (Evreinoff, 1970: 104). Recognizing theatricality, Evreinoff suggests, allows us actively to improve the world. 'If our life is a theater', he asks, 'why should we not make a really good theater out of it?' (Evreinoff, 1970: 111).

Although it never mentions Evreinoff, the sociologist Erving Goffman's study *The Presentation of Self in Everyday Life* (1959) lends the authority of careful observation to his claims about the ineluctable theatricality of life. Goffman argues that all social interactions are akin to performances, based on a fundamental division between the actor and audience, and between a self that potentially knows it is acting and the character it plays. The aim of these performances is to engender 'the impression of reality', to persuade an audience that the act is sincere (Goffman, 1959: 17). No less than for stage acting, the aim of social acting is mimesis. Failure to play a role, or playing it poorly, will come across as a breach in decorum. Goffman argues that the impression of reality is 'statistical' rather than intrinsic or necessary to the performance, since it arises from the belief of actor and audience in the role (1959: 71). At one extreme on this sliding scale is the con man, who does not believe his performance but elicits the belief of the audience. At the other extreme is, for example, the military officer, who has great faith in the performance of his or her duty. Such a performer, Goffman writes, believes that 'the impression of reality which he fosters is the one and only reality' (1959: 80). He is actor and audience at one and the same performance. Social interactions typically lack a formal script, but in the presence of others we alter our posture, facial expressions and tone of voice, to express our social status or position, just as actors do when they perform a role in the theatre. 'All the world is not, of course, a stage', Goffman writes, 'but the crucial ways in which it isn't are not easy to specify' (1959: 72).

Goffman's chief focus in his book is social establishments such as restaurants or department stores, in which space is organized between front-stage and back-stage regions, much as in theatres, and where 'teams' of employees perform for a small audience. But his most suggestive points concern the relationship between actor and role. Although we tend to believe that we are most 'ourselves' in private life, Goffman argues, somewhat like Shakespeare's Jaques, that there is no self apart from the various public roles we play. Selfhood is merely an effect of acting. 'A correctly staged and performed scene', he writes, 'leads the audience to impute a self to a performed character':

> but this imputation – this self – is a product of a scene that comes off, and is not the cause of it. The self, then, as a performed character, is not an organic thing that has a specific location, whose fundamental fate is to be born, to mature and to die; it is a dramatic effect arising diffusely from a scene that is presented, and the characteristic issue, the crucial concern, is whether it will be credited or discredited.
>
> (Goffman, 1959: 253)

Goffman here argues that the 'perceptual dynamics' of theatrical mimesis is at the bottom of the sense of self. Like theatre, selfhood is a product of the relationship between actor and audience, not an autonomous material reality. The public self is not a more or less authentic copy of a private original. Rather, the sense of an inner self is a copy generated by social performances. The self is a mere 'peg', in Goffman's words, on which roles of 'collaborative manufacture' are hung for a time (1959: 253).

Goffman is careful to note that his account of social performances characterizes British and American culture, and may not apply universally. But for the anthropologist Victor Turner, theatrical and dramatic forms are one of the crucial ways in which both traditional and modern cultures deal with conflict. Turner argues in a series of influential studies from the 1960s and 1970s that social conflicts follow a structure very similar to the tragic plots Aristotle describes in the *Poetics*. Like tragic dramas, what Turner calls 'social dramas' have a highly formalized structure, which can be broken down into four phases. The first phase is marked by the breach of a norm, in which someone or some group transgresses against morality, law or custom in a public arena. The breach is followed by a crisis, in which sides are taken and factions formed, and which may affect a small group or may spread to the entire culture. In the third phase, the leading members of the society bring adjustive or redressive mechanisms to bear on the crisis. In traditional cultures this may involve a ritual sacrifice or the intervention of tribal elders; in modern cultures, the mechanisms are often judicial or legislative. The social drama ends with what Turner calls reintegration: either the crisis is resolved or the parties accept a permanent cleavage (Turner, 1982: 70–1).

For Turner, nearly every conflict, from family disputes to murder trials and wars between nations, can be understood according to the model of the social drama. Theatre borrows and formalizes the structure of the social dramas, but it can also transform them. There is, Turner writes, 'an interdependent . . . relationship between social dramas and genres of cultural performance in perhaps all societies' (1982: 72). A theatrical performance may take a familiar social drama as its subject, as with a movie about a war or famous trial, but the participants in actual social dramas may likewise take cues for their behaviour from theatre. 'Life itself', Turner writes of such cues, 'now becomes a mirror held up to art, and the living now perform their lives'. The protagonists of a social drama, having been 'equipped by aesthetic drama with some of their most salient opinions, imageries, tropes, and ideological perspectives', perform their parts according to what they have learned from art and literature (Turner, 1982: 108). Although theatre is a distinct institution, the lines between social and aesthetic drama can never be drawn in advance. They both imitate the same dramatic structure and are part of the same never ending show that makes up life.

5

REALISM

THE GRAPES OF ZEUXIS

In his *Natural History* (77 CE), the Roman writer Pliny the Elder describes a competition between two of the greatest painters in ancient Greece, Zeuxis and Parrhasius. Zeuxis took the first turn, and produced a picture of grapes so successful that birds flew up to the place it was hung. Parrhasius then painted a picture of curtains, which was so realistic that Zeuxis, confident that he would win the competition, called out for the curtains to be drawn and Parrhasius' picture displayed. Having recognized his error, Zeuxis declares Parrhasius the victor, noting that 'whereas he had deceived birds, Parrhasius had deceived him, an artist' (Pliny, 1952: 311). This story is among the most famous fables about realism in Western literature, and it tells us a great deal about how the theory of mimesis has been understood. Much like Plato, who lived at roughly the same time as the two painters, Pliny assumes that the purpose of art is to mirror nature. Zeuxis believes himself to have succeeded when he fools birds with his painted grapes. Success for him means erasing the boundary between art and reality. Parrhasius' painting has no other aim than fooling Zeuxis. Both painters embody Plato's fear about the confusion mimesis sows in the soul of the viewer or reader. But they also epitomize the fascination of Western critical theory with the idea of artistic realism.

What makes a work of art or literature seem realistic to us? And why is realism so often held out as an ideal? Artistic realism is probably the most familiar element in the thematic complex of mimesis, but also one of the most controversial. 'At no time in the history of Western aesthetic theory', writes the German philosopher Hans Blumenberg, 'has there been any serious departure from the tendency to legitimize the work of art in terms of its relation to reality' (Blumenberg, 1977: 30). But this does not mean that the relationship between art and reality is static. Artists and writers since ancient Greece have, with few significant exceptions, struggled to provide an increasingly exact representation of reality, to improve both the medium of imitation and the techniques used to achieve it. At least that is the story Western art tells itself. The early advocates of perspectival techniques in the Renaissance claimed to provide an advance over the unrealistic productions of the 'dark ages'. Nineteenth-century novelists claimed to tell the truth about common people for the first time. Photography was presented as an advance over painting, motion pictures as an advance over still photography, and virtual reality as a quantum leap over film. Each technique has doubtless improved our ability to reproduce the world we see and experience. Yet this relentless artistic and technological quest for better ways of depicting reality is strangely fixated on traditional ideas about mimesis. Indeed, why should any art seek merely to reproduce the world we know through our senses? The realism of photography and film, we might suggest, is not an inevitable development, but the product of the Greek ideas about images that we have been tracing out in this book. We might go so far as to suggest that it is only because Plato defined art by its more or less accurate reproduction of the real that linear perspective or photography or virtual reality can be understood to mark progress in art, rather than just a change in medium or style.

Indeed, when placed in global and historical context, the Western devotion to realism is an exception rather than the rule. There are many other valid justifications for art than reproducing the real. Few cultures outside the West have regarded realism as an important goal. Motivated by the Biblical injunction against graven images, for example, many Islamic cultures strictly forbid the depiction of living human and animal forms in art. Traditional landscape painting in China and Japan is highly conventional in its depictions of nature, and often strikes Western viewers as abstract or artificial. Many traditional cultures, moreover, do not make the sharp distinction between art and reality that Western theory has inherited from Plato. Art in these cultures is closely intertwined with ritual or with daily life, much as it seems to have been in archaic Greek culture before Plato's intervention. Without the presumed difference of art from reality that underwrites Plato's critique of mimesis, the idea of realism, of reproducing life in a different medium, has little meaning. This is true historically as well. Medieval art was largely informed by a Christian rejection of the worldly, and thus tended to minimize the mimetic ideal handed down by Greek thought. What looked to many later commentators like a decline in artistic skill during the period can be attributed to a shift in the uses of and justifications for artistic production. It was not until the Renaissance revival of Greek art and philosophy that mimetic realism again became the chief aim of painters and sculptors.

Yet although it has constituted one of the central problems for Western art, realism is exceedingly difficult to define. It is perhaps for this reason that the novelist Henry James wrote of the 'air of reality' in the novel (1984: 53). Like air, we might suggest, realism is the very element of art in Western culture, but it is also invisible. It is a feeling, something we recognize when we encounter it, or miss when it is absent, rather than a single quality of any given work. In large part, the difficulty of defining realism lies in a crucial ambiguity of the word *real.* As the literary theorist Raymond Williams has noted, this word can have almost diametrically opposed senses. On the one hand, we often use real in opposition to the false or imaginary. The real is concrete and knowable to the senses. On the other hand, we also use real in opposition to appearances or to self-deceptive convictions. In this case, the real points to underlying or overlooked facts, to truths not apparent in everyday life. The real here is precisely what we cannot know by the senses or through material objects in the world (Williams, 1983: 258). We can add to these opposed definitions the notion of the real as practical. In political theory, this sense of realism describes a hard-nosed willingness to engage with things as they are, rather than striving for an 'unrealistic' ideal.

In art and literature, these varied senses of the real shift markedly according to who does the defining, and why. Because realism is both a general concept and the name of a specific movement in nineteenth-century art and literature (to which we shall return), it is easy to confuse the practice of particular artists with the broader philosophical problem of art after Plato. As the literary scholar René Wellek has written, '[a]rt cannot help dealing with reality' (1963: 224), but the nature of that reality is flexible. Dante, for example, claimed his *Divine Comedy* depicted the truest reality: the spiritual reality of life after death. His long poem leads its readers through the supernatural realms of hell, purgatory and paradise. By contrast, the nineteenth-century French realist Honoré de Balzac, who called his cycle of interrelated novels the *Human Comedy* in imitation of Dante's work, follows the scientific spirit of his age and, like other realists in the period, highlights the concrete interactions of common people and contemporary social life. Dante's real and Balzac's real are very different things, despite the fact that both writers claim the real as their major subject. Of course, no realist simply copies the given world, however much artists and writers may claim such a goal. Novelists invent characters and plots, painters frame and position their subjects, and documentary photographers manipulate shutter speed, exposure time and camera angle to achieve certain effects. Realism is an interpretation of mimesis, and thus generates potentially contradictory definitions.

Most of the criteria by which artists and critics have attempted to define realism are no more definitive than Dante's or Balzac's. It is often suggested, for example, that realism lies in a work's power of illusion. The most realistic work is the most deceptive, the one that best mimics appearances. This idea is implicit in Plato's comparisons of art to an optical illusion, or in Pliny's account of Zeuxis and Parrhasius. But as the philosopher Nelson Goodman points out, in *Languages of Art* (1968), there are few works, realist or not, that actually set out to fool the viewer. And even those that do (such as optical illusions) are marginal genres. Moreover, while we may be fooled momentarily by optical illusions, we do not confuse them with concrete reality for long. The reader of a realist novel or a museum-goer looking at even the most realistic painting is well aware that he or she is dealing with a work of art (Goodman, 1968: 34–5). It is also possible to attribute the realism of a work to both its subject matter and to its manner of presentation. Literary and artistic realism in the nineteenth century stressed the contemporary and the quotidian. It depicted common people doing everyday activities. But is this focus on everyday life essential to all realism? What is the status of the supernatural or the futuristic? Nineteenth-century realists rigorously avoided depicting supernatural events. But science fiction films rely on the possibility of depicting the supernatural or extraterrestrial in a realistic manner, epitomizing what film theorist Christian Metz calls cinema's unique power to 'realize' the unreal (1974: 5). By contrast, the novels of such twentieth-century Latin American 'magical realists' as Gabriel García Márquez fuse realistic depictions of people and society with patently supernatural or impossible events that are not treated as such by the characters. For both science fiction and magical realism, the sense of realism lies in the manner of presentation, which renders the unreal familiar or the real strangely unfamiliar.

The standard for determining realism can also change over time. This fact underscores the role of artistic intention and the expectations viewers or readers bring to a work. In his essay, 'On Realism in Art' (1921), the Russian linguist Roman Jakobson notes that realism can arise from either or both of these factors. The artist may or may not seek to give an accurate depiction of reality, and the viewer or reader may or may not judge the work to be realistic, regardless of what the artist intended. The impressionist paintings of Claude Monet, for example, seek to capture the play of light and colour in our perception of the world, but in so doing sacrifice the clear outlines and perspectival depth of most post-Renaissance art. Monet claimed to give a realistic rendering of his perception of things, and his supporters claimed that his works were more realistic than traditional paintings, but a viewer accustomed to older styles would find his works unrealistic. Rather than being an inherent property of the work, then, realism in this instance lies in a relationship between intention and reception, between the artist and the audience. '[O]nly those artistic facts which do not contradict my artistic values', Jakobson comments, 'may be called realistic' (1987: 23). Technological changes can have a similar effect on artistic values. Early responses to photography, for example, uniformly stressed its almost miraculous reproduction of life. Edgar Allan Poe compares the realism of photographs to objects 'reflected in a positively perfect mirror'

(Trachtenberg, 1980: 38). But Poe was writing about black and white photographs, which, since the development of colour and the mechanical and optical improvements in cameras since the nineteenth century, now seem quite unrealistic to us.

REFLECTION AND CONVENTION

Given the overriding complexities of defining the term, coming to a single useable definition of realism might seem impossible. The word can describe both subject matter and form of presentation, can apply to both verbal and literary works, and may depend on the potentially disparate judgements of author and viewer or reader. Such judgements can also change radically over time and across cultural contexts. Rather than seeking to define realism in the abstract, then, it is perhaps more fruitful to consider some of the ways realism has been defined by artists and critics. As always in the study of mimesis, it is helpful to go back to Plato and Aristotle, and to the two foundational poles for understanding mimesis and its relationship to human nature and culture, which I described in the introduction.

Plato, as we saw, is concerned above all with the uncanny power of art to mirror the material world. He criticizes mimesis for its inability to go beyond this kind of mirroring, for appealing only to the senses and not to reason, but in so doing he provides us with one major criterion of realism: the accurate reproduction of material reality. This is the notion of realism we tend to apply to photography, to detailed literary descriptions of people and places, and to perspectival painting, all of which purport to give the viewer or reader a faithful representation of the material world as it appears. For Aristotle, by contrast, the realism of a work is intellectual rather than strictly material. Aristotle stresses the importance of organizing the plot according to probability and necessity. Rather than seeking to reproduce the world as it is, mimesis 'matches' our innate or conventional ways of knowing the world. Realism occurs in the interaction of work and viewer (much like theatrical mimesis) and not of work and world. Since the Renaissance, this notion of realism has been termed verisimilitude, which defines the work as 'true to life' rather than as a replica of life. A work is realistic to the extent that it does not violate our conventional sense of authenticity, what Aristotle defines in terms of probability and necessity, even if it describes things that have never existed or would be impossible in reality.

Plato's 'reflection' theory and Aristotle's 'convention' theory have informed debates about artistic realism from antiquity to the present. Let us take, for example, discussions of realist style. Realism is often defined by its proponents as a lack of style and a rejection of conventions. It is reality presented directly and without distortion. Following this definition, realists in the nineteenth century compared themselves with scientists, and decried the reliance of past artists on imitation and tradition rather than personal observation. The nineteenth-century French writer Emile Zola, for example, described his novels as 'experimental'. And the French critic Fernand Desnoyers writes in his 1855 manifesto 'On Realism', 'I demand for painting and for literature the same rights as mirrors have' (Becker, 1963: 82). But the reflection theory of realism is belied by many instances of realist style. The example of film is especially instructive. Film is the contemporary epitome of realism for its ability to reproduce the physical world. But filmmakers often rely on familiar conventions when they want to signal the truthfulness of their work: grainy black and white footage, poor lighting, shaky hand-held cameras, distorted sound. These stylistic conventions give a sense of immediacy and 'eventness' to the scene, as if it were random and unrehearsed. As the art historian Linda Nochlin has noted, a similar group of conventions informed realist painting in the nineteenth century. One of the hallmarks of realism in art of the period was the implicit sense that the artist was reproducing 'the random, the changing, the impermanent and unstable' (Nochlin, 1971: 28). Realist subjects are often in motion, she observes, as if the picture were capturing a fleeting moment by mere chance, despite the fact that the subjects were carefully posed by the painter. Filmic conventions for signifying truth carry this nineteenth-century equation of the real with the random and fleeting into a new context. Instead of treating the camera as a mirror held up to the world, film here signifies truth conventionally by sacrificing the extreme fidelity of the medium.

Discussions of realist style have often identified the central importance of details and descriptions. Richness of detail is a hallmark of realism, but here, too, we find a division between reflection and convention theories. As Nochlin points out, the interest of nineteenth-century realists in concrete details, like so much else in the movement, was influenced by scientific methods (1971: 41). Details in realist works highlight the artist's observational fidelity. They seem random, arbitrary and unchosen, stressing the familiar association of the real with the fleeting. Yet the realist detail is also a highly conventional stylistic technique. Jakobson, for example, argues that realist details are based on a figure of speech called metonymy. Unlike metaphor, which compares dissimilar things, metonymy substitutes one thing for something associated with or close to it, such as saying 'crown' for 'king'. Realist metonymies create an entire world by way of such associations: one or two details imply the possibility of infinite details 'outside' the scene that might have been described. The realist author, Jakobson writes, 'metonymically digresses from the plot to the atmosphere and from the characters to the setting in space and time' (Jakobson, 1987: 111). He points to the example of the nineteenth-century Russian novelist Leo Tolstoy, who often identifies characters through physical features such as a bare shoulder or hair on the lip. The bare shoulder hints at an entire body, and then at an entire social context for which the shoulder might have a distinct erotic or moral significance. Metonymy in this instance is a convention that suggests the objectivity of the realist's observation and situates the work in a recognizable social world. In his essay, 'The Reality Effect' (1968), the French literary critic Roland Barthes goes even further, suggesting that the realistic detail is entirely a product of convention. Realist details, he argues, rely for their impact on the conceptual 'category of "the real"' rather than on reality itself (Barthes, 1986: 148). Unlike traditional symbols, Barthes suggests, realist descriptions seem concrete, particular and essentially meaningless in themselves. But the very insignificance of these details is telling, since the 'real', for Western culture, is always what resists meaning. The real is 'what is there' before human thought or action takes hold of it. Rather than being real, the insignificant detail paradoxically signifies reality conventionally by its appearance of insignificance.

The pervasiveness of the reflection–convention distinction in Western theory is best grasped in the visual arts. Since painting and sculpture in the mimetic tradition seem self-evidently to mirror the world, one would expect Plato's notion of realism to dominate the critical tradition surrounding them. To a great extent this is true, as Pliny's exemplary tale suggests. But there is also a running sense in discussions of painting that realism is as much about the skilful use of convention as the direct reproduction of nature. One of the most important realist techniques in the history of painting was the development of linear perspective in fifteenth-century Italy. Based on new theories of optics and geometry, perspective allowed painters to produce an illusion of three-dimensional space on the flat surface of the painting. For the founders of Renaissance perspective, painting seemed freed from outmoded conventions, and empowered to depict reality for the first time.

In his treatise, *On Painting* (1435), the Italian artist and architect Leon Battista Alberti, who first formalized this technique, compared the perspectival painting to a window. The surface of the image should seem 'transparent and like glass', as if the spectator were looking through it to the world on the other side (Alberti, 1991: 48). For Alberti, the two forms of seeing are identical. The eye, he argues, sends out a 'pyramid' of rays to the object. These rays are akin to 'very fine threads gathered tightly at one end' (Alberti, 1991: 40). The base of the pyramid is formed by the object seen, the apex is within the eye, and the sides are defined by the 'threads' running from the eye to the edges and the surface of the object. Perspectival construction is governed by the nature of this so-called 'visual pyramid'. Painters, Alberti argues, should imagine the surface of the work as a plane intersecting the pyramid at some point between the viewer and the spectacle. On one 'side' of the painted surface is the viewer, and on the other is the imaginary space in which the spectacle unfolds. The central 'vanishing point' of the work, towards which all lines in the painting converge, is determined by a perpendicular line running from the viewer's eye through the surface of the painting. This system for representation, Alberti claims, brings painting in line with 'the basic principles of nature' (1991: 37). Art is successful to the extent that it mimics vision and presents the viewer with nature as it appears to the eye.

Alberti's account of perspective was deeply influential, and for hundreds of years defined the standard of realism in painting. But many scholars have questioned Alberti's claim that perspective renders the world as it really is. As Erwin Panofsky argues, in his classic essay 'Perspective as Symbolic Form' (1924), the model of vision Alberti describes is based on two problematic assumptions: first, that we see with a single and immobile eye; and second, that a cross-section of the visual pyramid reproduces the optical image. Both of these assumptions, Panofsky argues, conflict with the actual workings of vision. We see, of course, with two eyes, which constantly scan what they perceive. And the field of vision is spherical, like the eye, not pyramidal. The flat surface of the painting and the straight lines of the visual pyramid are abstractions, conventional ways of describing vision that do not correspond to its actual nature. Panofsky also notes that other cultures have held very different ideas of artistic space. Alberti imagines space as homogeneous, measurable, and 'systematic' (Panofsky, 1997: 42), bringing art close to the kind of scientific study of the natural world that was also emerging at the time. Medieval painting, by contrast, uses space differently. Where Alberti's linear perspective regards space as a mere emptiness between figures, medieval artists tend to cover the pictorial surface with colour and detail, as one finds in church mosaics or the elaborate and colourful illustrations that decorate many medieval manuscripts. In the first context, artistic space is analogous to physical space, subject to rational analysis and objective description, while in the second, it is a flat surface to be filled with colour and designs. All artistic space is, for Panofsky, a set of conventions for representation, not a better or worse reproduction of real space or actual perception.

Taking Panofsky's conventionalist position even farther, Goodman argues that perspective is entirely a matter of 'reading' rather than seeing. It is a system whose rules need to be acquired and internalized. Perspectival paintings, Goodman notes, make unacknowledged and inconsistent choices about what distortions in vision to correct. According to the rules of perspective, railroad tracks, telephone poles or parallel joints in floor tiles running outwards from the eye will converge as they become more 'distant'. This illusion corresponds in most respects to actual vision. But in the same painting the edges of two facing buildings, which run upwards from the line of sight, will be depicted as parallel. Why correct one distortion and not the other? The choice is a matter of historically specific conventions, and not optics. Indeed, for Goodman, no painting ever 'resembles' nature. Pictures are self-evidently different from other objects, and thus symbolize or refer to such objects, rather than mirroring them. The difference between a realistic and an unrealistic representation lies in our familiarity with the conventions each work uses. 'Realism is a matter not of any constant or absolute relationship between a picture and its object', Goodman writes, 'but of a relationship between the system of representation employed in the picture and the standard system' of the time (1968: 38). Works seem realistic to us because the key to reading them is so commonplace that we do not recognize it as a key.

REALISM AND SINCERITY

We find a different version of the contrast between Platonic and Aristotelian notions of mimesis in discussions of nineteenth-century literature. Language corresponds less obviously to the material world than do the visual arts, so the differences between a reflection and a conventionalist account of realism in literature take a unique form. Most notably, they turn upon the sincerity of the author. Realist writers often stake their claim to mimetic fidelity on the honesty and objectivity of their aims rather than on the exact correspondence of the work to reality. Realism here is an ethical ideal. 'The sum and substance of literary as well as social morality', writes the American novelist Theodore Dreiser, 'may be expressed in three words – to tell the truth' (Becker, 1963: 155). The association of art with truth-telling redefines Plato's image of art as a mirror. Rather than blaming literature for seeking to mirror the world, realist writers redefine the mirror as a metaphor for the truthfulness of their project. Perhaps the most famous instance of this redefinition is the French novelist Stendhal's claim, in *Scarlet and Black* (1830), that:

> a novel is a mirror journeying down the high road. Sometimes it reflects to your view the azure blue of heaven, sometimes the mire in the puddles on the road below. And the man who carries the mirror in his pack will be accused by you of being immoral! His mirror reflects the mire and you blame the mirror! Blame rather the high road on which the puddle lies.
>
> (1953: 365–6)

For Stendhal, the mirror embodies the writer's impartial devotion to unvarnished truth. The realist novel seeks to mirror the world in all its variety, regardless of its possible affronts to traditional morality or accepted canons of beauty.

In a well-known passage from her novel *Adam Bede* (1859), George Eliot offers a similar defence of her own commitment to realism:

> I aspire to give no more than a faithful account of men and things as they have mirrored themselves in my mind. The mirror is doubtless defective; the outlines will sometimes be disturbed; the reflection faint or confused; but I feel as much bound to tell you, as precisely as I can, what that reflection is, as if I were in the witness-box narrating my experience on oath.
>
> (1996: 175)

Like Stendhal, Eliot redefines Plato's mirror as a metaphor for the truth of art, not its lies. Art is akin to legal testimony, which values honesty and accuracy over beauty, absolute truthfulness over decorum. Even more than Stendhal, Eliot shifts the criteria for success from the objective form of the work to the subjective intentions of the artist. The literary performance may introduce distortions in the work's depiction of reality, but the author's good intentions can still make it truthful. Eliot also compares her work to the 'truthfulness' of Dutch painting, which was long recognized (and often criticized) for faithfully reproducing the existence of common people. Rather than depicting 'prophets, sibyls, and heroic warriors', Eliot gives her readers everyday individuals with 'squat figures, ill-shapen nostrils, and dingy complexions'. Prophets and sibyls represent an ancient variety of truth-telling, but their revelations no longer evoke the 'delicious sympathy' with others that, Eliot maintains, the truthfulness of a realist novel can produce in its readers (Eliot, 1996: 177).

The focus among realist writers on honesty and truthfulness would seem to favour the Platonic over the Aristotelian theory of art. Although Stendhal and Eliot implicitly reject Plato's assertion of art's dishonesty, they nevertheless share his sense that literature can reflect reality. Yet it is primarily Aristotle's model that underlies two of the most important studies of literary realism in the twentieth century: Georg Lukács'

Studies in European Realism (1950), and Erich Auerbach's *Mimesis* (1946). Both critics believe, like the writers they discuss, that realism offers the most accurate and truthful depiction of the world as it is. But both also highlight the conventional methods that realist writers rely upon to achieve this aim.

For Lukács, the realist novel is the product of a specific moment of historical transition: the establishment of capitalism as an economic and political force. Balzac and Tolstoy stand above other realists, he claims, because they give vivid literary form to this historical moment. They grasp the importance of the changes going on around them, and seek to document them in literary form. They do so, Lukács notes, despite their own reactionary political beliefs: Balzac supported the declining French aristocracy, and Tolstoy was a mystical Christian. 'Balzac's greatness', Lukács writes, 'lies precisely in the fact that in spite of all his political and ideological prejudices, he yet observed with incorruptible eyes all the contradictions as they arose, and faithfully described them' (2002: 38–9). Much like Stendhal and Eliot, Lukács stresses the honesty, sincerity and objectivity that underlie nineteenth-century realism. Realism is defined by the aims and intentions of the artist, and not directly by the nature of the work itself.

Yet Lukács largely rejects the Platonic metaphor of the mirror for a more Aristotelian emphasis on the representation of plot and character. The objectivity that marks the works of Balzac and Tolstoy, he argues, should not be confused with a 'pedestrian copying of reality'. These works are 'absolutely true to life', but convey that truth in their attention to stories and relationships rather than the concrete details of material reality (Lukács, 2002: 43). Balzac, for example, reveals the social and economic forces driving his age by depicting the effects of social institutions through stories of personal relationships. He shows the real conflicts between class interests by detailing fictional conflicts among his characters. These characters are what Lukács calls 'types'. A type is neither average nor an allegorical embodiment of abstract ideas but a synthesis of the general and the particular. He or she is an individual personality, with a past history, passions and traits, but also a typical representative of his or her class. Thus we come to regard characters' actions as both the natural outcome of the characters' personalities and as a consequence of their class interests and the economic forces of history. The use of types, Lukács argues, allows realist writers to reproduce a social totality and mirror the intricate relationship between individual and social context that defines the age.

Lukács tellingly contrasts the realism of Balzac and Tolstoy with the next generation of French 'naturalist' writers, such as Zola and Gustave Flaubert. The naturalists found themselves in a changed social context, in which capitalism had become the dominant economic model and the bourgeoisie an uncontested political force. The social world seemed 'finished', a closed and static system that the writer could only observe as if from without. 'The writer no longer participates in the great struggles of his time', Lukács argued, 'but is reduced to a mere spectator and chronicler of public life' (2002: 89). The naturalist substituted meticulous descriptions for the realistic portrayal of human choice and conflict. Where the realists focused on social relationships, the naturalists attempted 'the direct, mechanical mirroring of the humdrum reality of capitalism' (Lukács, 2002: 93). And where the realists depicted a social totality through the selection of representative characters and incidents, the naturalists gave a chaotic mass of unconnected and disorganized details. Much like Aristotle, Lukács values the ability of a carefully designed plot to give the reader a glimpse of universal truths. The sense of reality comes not from a Platonic mirroring of the given world but from a purposeful ordering and presentation of fictional events.

Auerbach's *Mimesis* also defines realism in terms of the relationship between reflection and convention. But where Lukács sees realism as the product of a specific historical moment, Auerbach treats it as a perennial possibility in Western literature, which is only fully realized with the nineteenth-century novel. Auerbach begins the volume with a comparison between the depiction of reality in two ancient texts: Homer's *Odyssey* and the story of Abraham in the book of Genesis. Auerbach finds two different mimetic impulses at play in these texts. For Homer, everything that occurs is placed in the foreground. Characters give voice to their most private deliberations, and important places are described in great detail. Past and present, public and private, major and minor incidents are all cast in the same bright light. Homer represents things, Auerbach writes, 'in a fully externalized form, visible and palpable in all their parts, and completely fixed in the spatial and temporal relations' (1974: 6). The Biblical story of Abraham, by contrast, leaves much in darkness. There are no descriptions of setting or character, we are given little insight into Abraham's thoughts as he contemplates sacrificing his son, and even God does not reveal His intentions in demanding this sacrifice. For Auerbach, the lack of descriptive and psychological detail creates a sense of hidden complexities. The Biblical characters 'have greater depths of time, fate, and consciousness' than do the characters in Homer (Auerbach, 1974: 12). They seem embedded in a process of individual, historical and theological change.

Thus Auerbach identifies two kinds of realism, which roughly accord with what we found in Plato and Aristotle: the descriptive and sensory realism of Homer and the interior, psychological realism of the Bible. Whereas the classical tradition following Homer will insist on clarity, order and unity of representation, the Biblical tradition leads to psychological depth, uncertainty of meanings and the need for interpretation. Auerbach finds a significant social dimension in the two forms of realism. Homer's characters are noble, powerful and mythical. The characters in the Bible are important to their social group but largely poor and downtrodden. The modern realism that, in Auerbach's account, takes the lives and occupations of common people seriously is entirely foreign to the Homeric tradition, but it is native to the Biblical tradition, and in particular to Christianity. For much of Western literary history, the impulse toward realism is dominated by what Auerbach terms the classical separation of styles. This doctrine, which followed from the tradition of Homer, presumes that everything realistic in the modern sense can be represented only in comedy or pastoral. All serious and tragic literature should concern the wealthy and powerful. The notion of a tragedy about a peasant would have been absurd.

For the Christian tradition, by contrast, every life is wracked by profound conflicts of faith. Auerbach offers the example of Peter's denial of Christ in the Gospel narratives, which depicts a common person in an extraordinary circumstance, tragically divided between his devotion to Christ and fear for his personal safety. 'A scene like Peter's denial', Auerbach writes, 'fits into no antique genre. It is too serious for comedy, too contemporary for tragedy, politically too insignificant for history' (Auerbach, 1974: 45). This is not to say, however, that the Biblical tradition simply produces realism. Indeed, Christianity also tends to undermine the accurate portrayal of reality because, as I noted earlier, it denigrates the worldly existence that realism seeks to detail. Where it does depict actual lives, it is motivated by the polemical aim of demonstrating the pain and despair of mere bodily existence. This is what Auerbach terms Christian 'creatural realism', a realism of corporeal suffering. It is only with the realist novels of the nineteenth century that the two possibilities are united. French writers such as Balzac, Stendhal and Flaubert join the clarity and order of the classical tradition with the Biblical concern for the tragic possibilities of everyday life. Realist novels depict characters of every class with equal seriousness. Even the lowest figures can be the subject of tragic conflict. These novels also show their characters to be 'embedded in a total reality, political, social, and economic, which is concrete and constantly evolving' (Auerbach, 1974: 463). They come closer than any other literary form to the lived experience of their readers.

PYGMALION'S FOLLY: ANTI-REALISM

Both Lukács and Auerbach believe that Western literary realism reaches its zenith in the nineteenth-century novel. Although neither critic imagines that the novel can or should simply mirror the world, both claim that nineteenth-century realism offers unprecedented insights into the logic of historical change and the lives of common people. But there is also a long tradition in Western thought that is suspicious of the realistic ideals that Lukács and Auerbach champion. The most obvious figure in this tradition is Plato, who criticized art for its rendering of mere appearances rather than the purely rational forms. The Biblical prohibition on graven images has inspired generations of iconoclasts, who insist that representations of nature or the divine are a transgression against God's commandments. European literature is rife with stories about artworks that are too real or encroach in humorous or frightening ways on human life. If the pinnacle of art, following Plato and Aristotle, is the faithful representation of nature, it is not difficult to imagine a representation so real that it actually takes on life. In his epic poem the *Metamorphoses*, for example, the ancient Roman writer Ovid tells of the mythical sculptor Pygmalion, whose disdain for real women leads him to carve a woman of ivory. His skills are so great, though, that he is soon taken in by the illusion and falls 'in love / With his own workmanship' (Ovid, 1955: 242). The goddess Venus takes pity on him, and actually gives life to the statue.

Perhaps the most germane tradition of anti-realism for this chapter arises from the same nineteenth-century milieu as the realist novels of Stendhal and Eliot. Writers such as Charles Baudelaire in France and Oscar Wilde in England made a spirited effort in the later half of the nineteenth century to challenge the idea of and the theoretical justifications for realism in art and literature. They argued that the true aim of art is beauty, not the reproduction of reality. In a world where ugliness seemed on the rise, and beauty increasingly in retreat, realism was an affront to its audience and a betrayal of art itself. In his *Salon* of 1859, for example, Baudelaire claims that the realism of photography betrays the true aims of art. The unsophisticated multitudes, Baudelaire argues, believe art should be devoted to the 'the exact reproduction of Nature' (1965: 152). Photography answers this demand, and thus seems to be the epitome of artistic realism. But Baudelaire denies that technological progress amounts to artistic progress. Indeed, photography poses a grave danger to art. It is, he claims, 'art's most mortal enemy' (Baudelaire, 1965: 154). Baudelaire fears in particular that photographic realism will be seen as an end in itself, and not a mere tool for human creativity. As a means of preserving the tourist's memory or aiding the work of the astronomer or the naturalist, photography is a valuable invention. But art is the realm of the impalpable and the imaginary, Baudelaire argues. If they seek merely to satisfy the public's demand for the artistic reproduction of a familiar world, the poet and the painter give away what makes their productions unique. 'Each day', Baudelaire writes, 'art further diminishes its self-respect by bowing down before external reality; each day the painter becomes more and more given to painting not what he dreams but what he sees' (1965: 154). The more the public becomes accustomed to photography, the more it will confuse the aim of realism with the ideal of beauty that, for Baudelaire, properly defines the work of art.

In his dialogue, 'The Decay of Lying' (1889), Wilde develops Baudelaire's critique of photography into a challenge to the realist novel. For Wilde, realist sincerity reduces the unique powers of art to 'a morbid and unhealthy faculty of truth-telling' (Wilde, 1982: 294). Art should never be bound to reproducing the world as it is. Indeed, the power to transform and improve upon the world is what distinguishes art from life, and human creativity from natural instinct. Realism makes art ugly and subjects it to the external world; the best art, by contrast, reshapes the world according to the ideal of beauty. 'Art takes life as part of her rough material', Wilde's speaker Vivian claims, 'recreates it, and refashions it in fresh forms, is absolutely indifferent to fact, invents, imagines, dreams, and keeps between herself and reality the impenetrable barrier of beautiful style, of decorative or ideal treatment' (Wilde, 1982: 301). Repudiating this power, and giving life and nature the upper hand, as Wilde claims realism does, is to drive art into the wilderness. In place of realist sincerity, Wilde proposes a restoration of the artistic lie. The best lies, Vivian argues, are simply 'beautiful untrue things', created for their own sake, and not to deceive or mislead (Wilde, 1982: 320). Unlike realism, artistic lies make no claim to objectivity. They are honestly dishonest, naturally artificial, and seek only 'to charm, to delight, to give pleasure', not to reproduce the world. Wilde, much like Stendhal and Eliot, adapts Plato's critique of mimesis to his own ends. But rather than turning the possibility of realism into a metaphor for honesty, Wilde ironically joins Plato in asserting the insincerity of art.

Baudelaire and Wilde accuse realism of betraying the autonomy of art in its seeming refusal to go beyond the menial task of copying the material world. For more recent versions of anti-realism, the betrayals of realist art are much further reaching. Arising out of the heady theoretical milieu of 1960s' Paris, theorists such as Roland Barthes saw realism, much as Brecht saw traditional theatre, as an elaborate ruse for the preservation of the status quo. In his influential account of literary realism, *S/Z*, published in 1970, Barthes poses a rigorously conventionalist challenge to the belief shared by Lukács, Auerbach and writers such as Stendhal and Eliot that the realistic representation of everyday life can have positive ethical and political effects in the world.

For Barthes, all literature is woven out of codes that seem to represent reality only because we never recognize their conventionality. Much like Goodman, Barthes describes realism as a convention so familiar that it has come to seem natural. For this reason, realism is inherently insincere. Through a meticulous analysis of Balzac's novella *Sarrasine* (1830), Barthes argues that the 'classic' realist artist 'knows the code' rather than the world. He or she weaves an elaborate tissue of clichés and commonplaces that produces an impression of reflection by way of convention alone. This tissue strikes us as realistic not because it accurately reflects the world but because it matches our expectations. The 'life' that realism imitates, Barthes writes, is 'a nauseating mixture of common opinions, a smothering layer of received ideas' (1974: 206). It is what 'has *already* been read, seen, done, experienced' (Barthes, 1974: 20). For Barthes, realism is but one interpretation, one particular arrangement, of codes. In principle, the codes of a culture can go on infinitely, with one code leading by association to any number of other codes. Realism tries to 'jam' this play of connotation, to tie each code to a single referent. It is, in this regard, profoundly conservative. Realism claims that the stories it tells are a picture of unvarnished reality, but this claim only serves to reinforce the public's sense that the current social order is just as natural and true as the realist representation of it. Realism gives the public what it wants, flatters its narcissism by mirroring a familiar world, but thereby impoverishes its understanding of society and renders it insensible to manipulation by the powers that be.

Barthes' critique of realist mimesis is wide-ranging, but it returns often to the role of description in realist writing. As we have seen, richness of description is a cornerstone of realist mimesis. But Barthes traces the mimetic force of description to a form of dissimulation. Realist mimesis, he argues, relies on 'the pictorial code'. Barthes notes how often realist descriptions borrow from the visual arts, alluding to the model of landscape painting in setting a scene or to still life in detailing objects. But writers try to pass these coded descriptions off as genuine observations. The realist writer places an 'empty frame' around a continuum of objects, and thus 'transforms the "real" into a depicted (framed) object'. Having borrowed this frame from the visual arts, the writer must then 'de-depict' the view, '*remove* it from his picture', by putting it into language. The realist author moves not from the real to language but from pictorial to literary codes. 'Thus, realism', Barthes writes, 'consists not in copying the real but in copying a (depicted) copy of the real' (1974: 54–5). Like Plato, curiously, Barthes places literary mimesis at two removes from the real. Yet it is the realist aspiration to mimesis, and not art itself, that produces the deception. Language never mirrors the world, Barthes suggests, it only becomes deceptive when reader and writer tacitly collude in believing that it can. Barthes attacks our habitual beliefs about representation rather than the nature of representation itself.

But if Barthes tends more towards an Aristotelian than a Platonic account of realism, he is also critical of Aristotle's claim that the realism of mimesis resides in its correspondence to rational thought. Realist narrative relies on a 'pseudo-logic' that answers to our conventional assumptions about real actions rather than to reality itself. The foundational principle of realism, he writes, is that 'everything must hold together' (Barthes, 1974: 181). A narrative strikes us as realistic because its events are manifestly joined 'with a kind of logical "paste"' that establishes causal relationships between events or within a character's personality (Barthes, 1974: 156). Nothing happens in realist texts without some explanation, but as Barthes shows, these explanations are often mutually contradictory. For example, the character Sarrasine seems at some points in the novel to know Italian, and at other points not to know it. In each specific context, his knowledge or ignorance of Italian serves a narrative purpose, but together these purposes are at odds with each other. The narrative sacrifices the overall organic unity Aristotle identifies as the function of plot for ensuring the local continuity of actions at different points in the story. Concerned above all with making sure everything hangs together, Balzac acts like 'an individual afraid of being caught in some flagrant contradiction' (Barthes, 1974: 156). He uses every trick in the book to ensure that his narrative maintains a sense of continuity, and thus to sustain the ruse that the conventions it weaves together are a truthful depiction of the world.

Whether it is governed by convention or reflection, is sincere or deceptive, the pinnacle or the decline of art, realism epitomizes the continuing influence that Plato and Aristotle hold over Western art theory. Debates over realism are part of the long shadow cast by the theory of mimesis. Realism, for this tradition, is not one artistic possibility among others but an unavoidable imperative that artists and critics either choose to obey or pointedly resist. Despite the difficulties of defining it, and despite the efforts of sceptics such as Wilde and Barthes to question its claims, realism remains the central interpretation of mimesis for modern culture.

PART THREE

Mimesis in Modern Theory

6

MIMESIS AND IDENTITY

PSYCHIC MIMESIS

I have suggested throughout this book that mimesis has always been at once a theory of art and an explicit or implicit theory of human nature. Accounts of mimesis in art rely on ostensible truths of human nature, and art is commonly regarded as an exemplary instance of an inherent human tendency towards imitation. This association of art and human nature informs both critiques and defences of mimesis. Plato's attack on mimesis begins with the problem of childhood education, and persistently links mimesis with extremes of human emotion. Aristotle defends mimesis according to many of the same psychological and anthropological criteria that Plato uses to discredit it. The instinct for imitation is 'implanted in man from childhood' and underlies the pleasure even adults gain from representations (Aristotle, 1951: 15). The final two chapters of this book explore how these ancient ideas about the interrelation of mimesis and human nature informed psychologists, sociologists, anthropologists and theorists of race and gender in the nineteenth and twentieth centuries. In this chapter, I will focus on psychoanalytic theories of identification, a term that describes the unconscious imitations of others that shape human identity. The concept of identification is central to the work of Sigmund Freud, the Viennese psychologist whose theories had a profound impact on Western thought in the early twentieth century and continue to inform current discussions of race and gender identity. In the final chapter, I will turn to theorists who study mimesis as an anthropological and cultural concept.

Nearly all of the theorists we shall discuss in these chapters regard mimesis as a primary aspect of human life, not a secondary or derivative imitation of something else. They uncover the mimetic origins of identity, and compare human collective life to the instinctual imitative behaviour of insects and animals. These theories reanimate a powerful set of questions about human nature that Plato first raised in the *Republic*, what Lacoue-Labarthe calls, in his essay 'Typography' (1975), the problem of 'fundamental mimetology'. This term describes the possibility that there is no single human nature, no unified self, but only a 'pure and disquieting *plasticity* which potentially authorizes the varying appropriation of all characters and all functions (all the roles)' (Lacoue-Labarthe, 1998: 115). Human existence is but a series of copies without a true original. As Philippe Lacoue-Labarthe notes, Plato begins his discussion of mimesis by noting the remarkable malleability of a child's mind, its ability to take on whatever 'stamp' one wants to give it, but he soon narrows the discussion to the nature of mimesis in art and poetry. The tradition of commentary that Plato inspired tends to start where Plato leaves off, assuming the close relationship between mimesis and human nature without taking up the potentially disturbing implications about identity that Plato raises and then seeks to curtail. Yet the long association of mimesis with acting, illusion and extreme emotions betrays a continuing anxiety about these implications. Lacoue-Labarthe identifies a line of theorists, from Plato to Diderot and Freud, who, in contrast to such traditional accounts, explore the mimetic bases of human thought and action. This interest in 'fundamental mimetology' informs many of the recent theories of mimesis we shall discuss as well.

Although, as Lacoue-Labarthe reminds us, the return to the psychology and anthropology of mimesis among twentieth-century thinkers is entirely consistent with the Platonic tradition, it has its immediate origins not in aesthetic theory but in a renewed interest in scientific and sociological theories of imitation among nineteenth-century thinkers. Inspired by Charles Darwin's writings on evolution from the 1850s, and by a contemporary fascination with hypnotism and other forms of psychological influence, many of the leading social theorists of the period came to define imitation as a foundational human behaviour. No less pivotal were the writings of Karl Marx (1818–83) and Friedrich Nietzsche (1844–1900), who explored the unconscious forces and unquestioned assumptions that shape everyday life. Although neither Marx nor Nietzsche makes mimesis a central category of his work, both of them identify the myriad ways in which human actions repeat patterns of behaviour inherited from the past or absorbed from the larger social context. For both philosophers, our lives are governed by conventional imitations that pass for facts of nature. As we shall find, this notion underlies nearly all of the important twentieth-century approaches to mimesis. Modernity presents itself as a liberation of the individual from tradition and social constraints, but in a striking variety of ways the theory of mimesis in the twentieth century implies that what look like autonomous actions and choices are really forms of imitation.

Among the most important psychological theorists of mimesis in the later nineteenth century, and an influence on Freud's thought, was the French sociologist Gabriel Tarde. In his major work, *The Laws of Imitation* (1890), Tarde defines imitation as a fundamental life force, one of the three great forms of 'universal repetition' that organize physical, biological and social life: 'imitation plays a rôle in societies analogous to that of heredity in organic life or to that of vibration among inorganic bodies' (Tarde, 1962: 11). Tarde has an expansive notion of imitation, which encompasses everything from the use of language to the spread of influential ideas, the institution of manners and even contagious laughter. Memory and habit are also forms of imitation. Engaged in either, we in fact imitate ourselves, instead of another person: memory recalls a mental image, much as habit repeats an action. Indeed, 'wherever there is a social relation between two living beings, there we have imitation' (Tarde, 1962: xiv). Whether we imitate willingly (following a fashion trend) or unwillingly (contagious laughter), we experience 'the action at a distance of one mind upon another' (Tarde, 1962: xiv). Tarde suggestively compares social imitation to hypnotic suggestion. 'Both the somnambulist and the social man', he writes, 'are possessed by the illusion that their ideas, all of which have been suggested to them, are spontaneous' (Tarde, 1962: 77). Ancient societies imitate their ancestors or their gods. In modern societies, people imitate each other. What we take to be original and individual choices are really the product of suggestion.

Yet Tarde does not regard civilization as a mere echo chamber, for imitations, he argues, tend towards greater complexity as they move through different social networks. Manners become more refined, languages more expressive, artistic traditions richer. For Tarde, 'nothing in history is self-creative' (1962: 150). All inventions and discoveries come from prior imitations. Tarde also regards imitation as socially progressive. Imitation begins in the family, where the father is a model for his children, but it soon spreads beyond the hierarchical structure of reproduction and inheritance. Whereas monarchies mime the pattern of the family, in which everyone imitates the model (father or ruler) in all of his or her qualities, democracies are defined by the partial and reciprocal imitation of many people. Everyone is allowed to imitate everyone else, and each individual can imitate different aspects of other groups or individuals. Imitation becomes an invisible and equalizing social bond that provides individuals with the means for greater personal expression: 'the very nature and choice of these elementary copies, as well as their combination, expresses and accentuates our original personality' (Tarde, 1962: xxiv). Even in its very structure, imitation tends towards personal and political freedom: 'through assimilating themselves with their models, the copies come to equal them, that is, they become capable of becoming models in their turn' (Tarde, 1962: 367). If allowed to flourish, imitation will unite individuals and nations into 'a single peaceful human family' without consequential differences of race, class, gender or privilege (Tarde, 1962: xxxiii).

IDENTIFICATION: FREUD

Although he only rarely uses the traditional vocabulary of mimesis and generally disavowed the influence of nineteenth-century theories of imitation on his own ideas, Freud took up and powerfully developed Tarde's suggestion that imitation is everywhere in human psychic life. For Freud, even our most deliberate thoughts and actions are governed by unconscious memories and desires. We reproduce aspects of our past in our everyday relationships with others, as well as in our dreams at night. The aim of psychoanalysis is to give patients an understanding of the unconscious forces that govern their behaviour, and thus to give them some perspective on the ways in which our present unwittingly imitates a repressed past. Freud was also a careful reader of Aristotle, and called his earliest therapeutic technique the 'cathartic method', because it sought to purge a patient's painful memories through hypnosis. Yet it is with the notion of identification that he most decisively rethinks both ancient and current theories of mimesis. According to this notion, the self arises from an unconscious imitation of others. Selfhood and identity are not given at birth, but comprise a mimetic amalgam of those who have influenced the ego, Freud's term for the sense of self. The French theorist Mikkel Borch-Jacobsen writes that identification is 'perhaps *the* fundamental concept . . . of psychoanalysis' (1988: 10). It informs Freud's account of dreams, childhood development, hysteria, artistic response, homosexuality and the formation of social groups, and as we shall find, it has remained important for theorists of identity, even as many other ideas Freud promoted have fallen out of favour.

Freud defines identification as 'the earliest expression of an emotional tie with another person' (1953–74: XVIII, 105). It describes the way in which one ego assimilates itself to another, and internalizes this role model as a pervasive ideal. Identification, Freud writes, 'endeavours to mould a person's own ego after the fashion of the one that has been taken as a model' (1953–74: XVIII, 106). Freud associates identification with the earliest stages of human development, and even goes so far as to claim that what we call character or personality might be nothing more than the history of our abandoned identifications (1953–74: XIX, 29). We are the people we have imitated. Freud stresses that identification is largely unconscious, and that this quality is what differentiates it from admiration, empathy, influence or other consciously recognized emotional bonds, and makes it both the origin of identity and the potential origin of neurotic symptoms. Borch-Jacobsen contrasts the Freudian self, in this regard, with the idea of the actor for Diderot and Brecht, which we discussed in chapter 4. Although our identity comes from the accumulated roles we borrow from others, there is, for Freud, no external standpoint from which we can observe our performance. Unlike actors, who intentionally manipulate the conventions of theatrical representation either to fool or to illuminate an audience, the Freudian ego is 'a mime through and through ... literally possessed by [its] role' (Borch-Jacobsen, 1988: 33).

The most important identifications are those we form as children. Childhood identifications follow the pathways of physical and emotional dependence, and thus focus on parents. The twentieth-century French psychoanalyst Jean Laplanche describes this sort of identification as 'structuring', and Freud sometimes calls it 'primary'. As we shall see later, such identifications fundamentally and irreversibly form the individual, if only because our parents are the first and most significant role models of our lives. In other telling contexts, such as hysteria and the formation of groups, identifications tend to be what Laplanche calls 'transitory' (1976: 80). These identifications come and go, and generally leave the core of the self unchanged. Transitory identifications form on the basis of a perceived common quality. Joining a group, for example, entails far more than sharing intellectual or political interests. We are unconsciously drawn to certain types of people or social situations, and accordingly come to imitate other members of the group in a variety of ways. We might begin to dress like others in the group, take on their ways of speaking and model our lives on the pattern of its most influential members. In most cases, such transitory identifications are harmless, but in extreme instances, such as mob violence or religious cults, they can become dangerous.

While identifications with a group involve adopting new forms of identity, other identifications follow upon the loss of something or someone. Freud first observed this process, which he called introjection, in cases of pathological mourning and depression. The ego here internalizes an emotional bond it has been forced to give up, and refashions itself on the model of the lost object as compensation. Imitation is a means of preserving a lost ideal, somewhat as it was for the Renaissance writers we discussed in chapter 3. Freud gives the suggestive example of a child who, unhappy over the death of a pet kitten, 'declared straight out that now he himself was the kitten, and accordingly crawled about on all fours, would not eat at table, etc' (1953–74: XVIII, 109). The child's introjection of the lost kitten, Freud implies, is more than a game. It acts like an entirely new structuring identification, transforming the child into an imitation of the object he has lost. This is an atypical case, however. More often, introjection divides the ego against itself. One part of the ego 'becomes' the lost object, takes up its voice and personality, much as the child becomes a kitten. Thus we might internally 'hear' the critical or supportive commentary of an influential friend, relative or teacher when we are making a choice. Such introjections can become pathological when the part of the ego that has been transformed by identification turns against the other part, and assails it in the name (and voice) of the lost ideal. Freud found this kind of internal division in cases of severe depression, in which patients commonly subject themselves to pathological self-criticism.

Freud's earliest uses of the concept of identification arose from his work with hysterical patients. Hysteria is the name for a now-discredited diagnostic category that was prevalent in nineteenth-century Europe and America. Hysterics, who were almost invariably women, would suffer physical symptoms, such as unexplained paralysis in a limb or a severe nervous cough, without evident organic causes. Hysterics were long known for their theatricality and remarkable powers of imitation. The nineteenth-century French physician Jean-Martin Charcot, with whom Freud studied, would stage public shows at his Parisian hospital, the Salpêtrière, in which hysterical patients 'performed' their symptoms for an audience. Freud himself writes, in *The Interpretation of Dreams* (1900), that hysterics can reproduce the symptoms of everyone around them, and in effect 'act all the parts in a play single-handed' (1953–74: IV, 149).

Hysterical imitation was most often explained as a 'psychical infection': one patient observes the symptom of another patient and imitates it with her own body. But for Freud, it arises from a complex unconscious process of identification. Freud gives the example of a patient in a mental hospital who suffers a hysterical attack after receiving a letter that reminds her of an unhappy love affair. The other patients who imitate her symptom do not simply reproduce its physical manifestations, but mimic the entire process of symptom formation. They unconsciously form an analogy between this woman's romantic past and their own, and reason that they too would succumb to the same symptom given the same cause. They copy the suffering woman's symptom based on the possibility, or even the unacknowledged desire, of receiving a disturbing letter. 'Thus identification', Freud writes, 'is not simple imitation, but *assimilation* on the basis of a similar aetiological pretension' (1953–74: IV, 150). In other words, rather than merely imitating the physical manifestations of the symptom, the hysteric imitates its psychological causes. This process of reasoning involves more than pity for the suffering patient. Indeed, fellow feeling is a result of identification, not its cause: 'a path leads from identification by way of imitation to empathy' (Freud, 1953–74: XVIII, 110). We sympathize with those who correspond to our identifications, rather than identifying with those whom we pity.

As these examples suggest, identification entails a potentially radical rethinking of mimesis. All of the theories of mimesis we have discussed assume that the artist intentionally imitates nature or a role model. For Freud, however, identifications are akin to an unconscious script that we unwittingly 'perform' throughout our lives. We incessantly imitate others, but not always by choice. Freud suggests that normal identifications are no less unwitting than those of the hysterics in the hospital ward or the little boy who became his dead kitten. Indeed, we never choose our most significant role models. Freud's follower Otto Fenichel puts it this way: 'When we make an identification we know nothing about it and we resist any clarifying insight' (1954: 100–1). Our relationships to others are governed by mimetic bonds over which we have little conscious control. As the literary critic Diana Fuss has noted, Freud's metaphors for identification often refer to impersonal forces such as gravity and infection (1995: 13). Identification installs an uncanny trace of otherness at the heart of identity, so much so that we can be surprised by the direction, intensity or emotional character of our identifications. Abandoned mimetic bonds can be revivified in new circumstances, casting a shadow over our present interactions. We may find ourselves habitually attracted to people with the same character or physical traits, or we may realize retrospectively that careers or hobbies we thought were freely chosen are in fact imitated from people with whom we once identified. Identifications often surface in seemingly insignificant gestures, catch-phrases and vocal intonations, and because we can maintain conflicting identifications at the same time, we may struggle with entrenched feelings that go conspicuously against more conscious convictions.

Perhaps the best example of the pull that unconscious identifications exert over our lives is the way most of us become increasingly like our parents as we grow older. Despite the influence of education, work and other intense emotional relationships, our earliest structural identifications continue to shape us even, perhaps especially, when we do not recognize – or when we actively seek to resist – their power. For this reason, the parent–child relationship is central to Freud's account of identification. Freud argues that children follow a universal pattern in their social and sexual development, which he calls the Oedipus complex, after the story of Aristotle's favourite tragedy, Sophocles' *Oedipus the King*. The young boy (Freud's default example) develops an intense identification with his father: 'he would like to grow like him and be like him, and take his place everywhere' (Freud, 1953–74: XVIII, 105). His father becomes an ideal, and the boy moulds his ego on him. Alongside this identification with the father, the boy also develops a desire for his mother. As Freud puts it, the boy wants to *be* his father, and to *have* his mother. Freud argues that desire and identification cannot coexist in the same attachment. Recent theorists have challenged this claim, because it renders homosexuality, in which one desires a person with whom one might also identify, a mere aberration. But for Freud, the conflict between desire and identification explains a curious moment in childhood development. Sometime between the ages of three and five years old, Freud observed, the boy comes to regard his father as a rival who thwarts his desire for the mother. Taking the father's place means replacing him in his relationship with the mother. As Freud points out, in this regard, identification is always ambivalent. It produces different emotions in different contexts, and 'can turn into an expression of tenderness as easily as into a wish for someone's removal' (Freud, 1953–74: XVIII, 105).

In the course of development, Freud argues, the bonds of identification and desire fix the child's sexual identity. Boys who identify strongly with their fathers become highly masculine, and girls who identify with their mothers become highly feminine. As the child grows, other men and women come to stand in for the parents, taking their place as role models or objects of desire. This outcome is what Freud called the 'positive' Oedipus complex. Freud came to recognize, however, that the play of desire and identification can be more fluid than this model dictates. Because Freud believes that all children are originally bisexual, the Oedipus complex can also have a 'negative' form, in which the child identifies with the parent of the opposite sex. This is one of the ways Freud, controversially, explains the origins of homosexuality: the boy identifies with his mother and desires men in imitation of her. The negative version of the Oedipus complex does not always result in homosexuality, however. It is common for young girls to identify with their fathers and become tomboys. In most cases, Freud suggests, this identification is temporary, and in adolescence the girl again takes her mother and other women as role models and men as objects of desire. Recent theorists of gender have criticized many of Freud's assumptions about sexual development, such as his assertion that there are normal and abnormal, 'positive' and 'negative' forms of identification. As we shall see, however, they have also developed and refined his insight that sexual identifications can be fluid and highly mobile.

The identifications that, according to Freud, mark the child's sexual development also have a decisive social and moral effect throughout life. After the passing of the Oedipus complex, children come, in Freud's words, to identify with 'the parental agency', rather than with the parents themselves (1953–74: XXII, 62). Having lost the parents as primary objects of desire or identification, the child, like the mourner, introjects their love and authority. They live on as an internal critical voice, what Freud calls the super-ego. The super-ego is the 'heir' to the Oedipus complex, and makes the originally ambivalent identification with his or her parents a permanent part of the child's personality (Freud, 1953–74: XXII, 162). It becomes the voice of conscience, and major source of guilt, and brings about the sense that some authority always observes and judges our actions from within. The idea of the super-ego also explains how groups form around strong leaders. The members of the group each identify with the leader and internalize him or her as their 'ego ideal'. The charismatic leader displaces the parents in the individual's psyche and takes over as the internal voice of approval or criticism. The follower identifies with and imitates the leader much as he or she had previously done with the parental agency.

THE MIRROR STAGE: LACAN

Freud's theory of identification has been enormously suggestive to theorists interested in subjectivity and identity, especially to scholars working on film and on questions of gender, race and sexual orientation. Although these theorists are often critical of Freud's conclusions, the notion that the ego is fashioned by mimetic relationships has become a foundational insight. Identification 'decentres' the ego by tracing its origins to external role models. It suggests that selfhood and identity are socially constructed, a product of what we see and whom we imitate rather than fixed or inevitable qualities. Recent theorists have also discerned an important political aspect to the notion of identification. If identity is constructed rather than given at birth, theorists gain a powerful means of challenging those beliefs, such as racism, sexism and homophobia, that regard difference as an essential and irremediable flaw.

Perhaps the key figure to stress this quality of identification was the French psychoanalyst Jacques Lacan, who produced his most influential works in the 1950s and 1960s. Lacan drew attention to a paradox in Freud's account of childhood development. If identification is the origin of the self, the model we imitate in shaping our personality and choices, who (or what) comes before the primordial choice of a role model? Can we even speak of a 'who' before this choice? As Borch-Jacobsen notes, Freud never clearly explains how identification begins or what comes before the first structuring act of imitation: 'In the beginning is mimesis: as far back as one goes . . . one always finds the identification from which the 'subject' dates' (1988: 47). Is there some unconscious self 'before' the ego that knows, for example, that boys should identify with their fathers rather than with their mothers, siblings or stuffed animals? Freud obliquely addresses this problem in his account of hysterical imitation, since hysterics 'choose' their role models unconsciously. This idea explains why children tend to identify with the parent who most resembles them physically. But this account begs the question of how the child knows this particular resemblance is relevant and leaves the primordial identification that structures the self largely unexplained. Where and how, then, does the chain of imitations that defines selfhood begin?

Lacan's influential answer, in an essay entitled 'The Mirror Stage as Formative of the Function of the I' (1949), was to posit a literally mimetic moment at the origin of the ego. Before the child identifies with its parents, Lacan suggests, it identifies with an image of itself. This primordial identification is what Lacan calls the 'mirror stage'. Lacan notes that, between the age of six and eighteen months, human infants begin to recognize themselves in a mirror. Unlike young chimpanzees, who lose interest in their mirror image quickly, infants remain fascinated with the reflection and respond to it with 'a flutter of jubilant activity' (Lacan, 1977: 1). For Lacan, this response indicates an act of identification. Lacan describes it as 'the transformation that takes place in the subject when he assumes an image' – or as he prefers to call it, an *imago* (1977: 2). Where Freud regards identification as an emotional tie between two people, Lacan treats it as a mimetic relationship between the still-undeveloped ego and its mirror image. Before children can identify with and imitate their parents or other role models, they have to identify reflectively with themselves. Lacan in this way returns the theory of identification to its origins in the mimetic tradition, and in explicit acts of imitation.

The process Lacan outlines is at once physical and psychological. Infants lack full control over their bodily functions and are dependent on others. Their inner sense of physical being is one of 'turbulent movements' (Lacan, 1977: 2): flailing limbs, lack of speech, inability to control their bodily functions. The image in the mirror, by contrast, appears unified, coherent, fixed and autonomous. It mimetically 'anticipates' for the infant a future physical maturation of its body. This anticipation is not just a wish but also an event that has consequential effects of its own. Lacan argues that the mirror image of physical unity 'symbolizes the mental permanence of the *I*' (1977: 2). It depicts the outer self as real and enduring, and in this way actually produces the unified ego. The image here comes before the properly established 'I' that recognizes it, the identification before the ego that identifies, the copy before the original. It shows the infant where it will be, and in doing so, actually forms the self it anticipates. It is only after the mirror stage that the ego is determined socially by its identification with its parents and, most decisively for Lacan, the 'symbolic order' of kinship laws, language, gender relations and other cultural formations.

Lacan seems well aware that his account of development reverses the traditional relationship between copy and original. Indeed, he points repeatedly to the artistic foundation of selfhood. The most obvious example is Lacan's tacit allusion to the myth of Narcissus, who falls in love with an image of himself reflected in a pool of water. Like Narcissus, the ego comes to know and love itself through a reflection, and thereby regards the world from 'a fictional direction' (Lacan, 1977: 2). Lacan also highlights the specifically aesthetic impact of the infant's primordial identification, referring to the imago as a 'statue', and suggesting that one finds lingering traces of the infant's original sense of bodily fragmentation in the art of the fifteenth-century Flemish painter Hieronymus Bosch, who often depicted scenes of bodily violence, and in the common literary theme of the double, where the protagonist confronts a mysterious duplication of herself (1977: 2). He also describes the mirror stage as a 'drama' that 'decisively projects the formation of the individual into history' (Lacan, 1977: 4). Lacan similarly underscores the engendering function of the mirror image in his use of scientific terminology and examples. Referring to the imagery of the laboratory, for example, he describes the mirror stage as the means by which 'the *I* is precipitated in a primordial form', almost as if it were the product of a chemical reaction (Lacan, 1977: 2). He compares the 'precipitation' of the self to the fact that female pigeons lack the organs of sexual reproduction until they see another member of their species, whether male or female. Like the gonads of a female pigeon, Lacan suggests, the ego is a social product, a result of our encounters with others, and not something present from birth.

Lacan's account of the mirror stage has a distinct polemical edge, as the analogy of the ego with the sexual organs of a pigeon suggests. Lacan is opposed to the modern philosophical notion of the ego as the autonomous and self-engendered centre of being, the stable point from which the outside world can be surveyed and mastered theoretically. Instead, drawing out the implications of Freudian identification, he highlights the ways in which the self is constructed by its relationship to the world and to others, first by seeing its own image and then by the influence of language and culture. The image in the mirror is not evidence of a pre-existing self, but the means by which it is produced. Lacan describes the effects of the image, in this regard, as 'orthopaedic' (1977: 4). But the ego misrecognizes its humble origins. Born premature and unable to communicate or care for itself, the human being is always compensating for its original dependence on others. It thus takes on 'the armour of an alienating identity' to set itself apart from the outside world (Lacan, 1977: 4). Lacan traces the origin of the neuroses in part to our aggressive policing of the boundaries of the self, our refusal to accept the influence of language, culture and unconscious forces on personal identity. He also hints at a subtle explanation for Plato's claim that there is a basic human susceptibility to mimesis. Unlike the young chimpanzee, which loses interest in the mirror when 'the image has been mastered and found empty', the child continues to stare (Lacan, 1977: 1). The mirror stage, Lacan implies, is never surmounted. Because the self originates in an image, it returns to the image as an abiding symbol for its autonomy, an ironically mimetic means of asserting our independence from mimesis.

PERFORMING RACE AND GENDER

Lacan's rethinking of identification as a form of mimesis was influential in literary and cultural theory throughout the 1970s and 1980s, especially through the writings of the French Marxist Louis Althusser. In his influential essay, 'Ideology and Ideological State Apparatuses' (1970), Althusser suggests that the mirror stage is social and political from the very start. By contrast with Marx, who defines ideology as an illusory or false representation of the world (see chapter 7), Althusser defines it as 'the imaginary relationship of individuals to their real conditions of existence' (1971: 162). It is an unconscious structure of identification, in which we recognize ourselves and others as free and willing 'subjects' of the prevailing social order. Much as the mirror stage constitutes us psychologically, so ideology constitutes us socially and politically, inculcates the underlying presuppositions about selfhood and identity with which we habitually operate.

Current theorists of race, gender and sexuality have likewise followed Freud and Lacan (and, in many cases, Althusser) in discerning the mimetic foundations of identity. Race, gender and sexual orientation might seem self-evidently fixed and given at birth, yet there is also a strong 'performative' element to the lived experience of identity. As the French philosopher Simone de Beauvoir famously wrote, 'One is not born a woman, but, rather, becomes one' (1973: 301). This dictum might describe all our various identities, for we are not simply men or women, gay or straight, black or white. Instead, these identities call on us to play a role that extends far beyond physical features or forms of desire. One must 'be a man', or 'act like a lady', as if gender were an ideal one needed to reach rather than an underlying biological truth. Racial identity is also a kind of performance, going far beyond skin colour to encompass such apparently incidental traits as clothing and hairstyle, ways of walking, gestures and language use.

Race and gender identity, in this regard, are very much effects of imitation. Just as Renaissance poets drew from a familiar constellation of literary conventions, so the clothes we wear, the way we talk and the manner in which we behave in public or in the bedroom are all imitated from an anonymous cultural repertoire. It is only because this repertoire is so familiar that, like a realist painting, it seems to be an unproblematic imitation of an underlying biological truth. What seems most natural about us is fundamentally conventional. But this is not to say that one can simply change races at will. Like gender, race is what the influential American philosopher Judith Butler calls a 'compulsory performance' that legitimates a hierarchical system of power and privilege (Butler, 1991: 24). One need only note how different it is for a man to dress as a woman or a white person to wear blackface than it is for a woman to disguise herself as a man or a black person to 'pass' as white. In the first set of examples, the inherent privilege of masculinity and whiteness makes the performance of femininity or blackness at best parody and at worst sexist or racist. In the second set of examples, by contrast, the disguise secures privileges that would otherwise be denied.

One of the first modern theorists to explore the ways in which gender identity is a performance was the psychoanalyst Joan Riviere. In an essay called 'Womanliness as a Masquerade' (1929), Riviere narrates the case history of an intellectual woman who used the trappings of femininity as a defence against anxiety. After every public speech she delivered, this woman would compulsively flirt with men who had been in the audience. Riviere traces the woman's intellectual interests to an Oedipal identification with her father. Rather than trying to take her father's place with her mother, though, she takes his place in public. The woman's compulsive flirtation, according to Riviere, is an unconscious attempt to ward off her father's anticipated retribution for her imitation.

The defensive performance of womanliness makes her intellectual work seem a mere joke, and thus not a threat to her father or other men. This kind of self-depreciating act has become familiar to researchers studying the intellectual development of adolescent girls, who often hide their intelligence to avoid intimidating boys. For Riviere, it raises larger questions about the nature of femininity: 'The reader may now ask how I define womanliness or where I draw the line between genuine womanliness and the "masquerade". My suggestion is not, however, that there is any such difference; whether radical or superficial, they are the same thing' (1991: 94). For the woman Riviere analyses, the attributes of femininity 'could be assumed and worn as a mask'. But this relation to womanliness is the norm rather than an aberration. Womanliness in every instance is not a mimetic reflection of biological sexual traits but a theatrical mask one dons as a defensive strategy. It is an artefact of identification, a social rather than a biological imperative.

Although Riviere regards her patient's feminine masquerade as a form of pathology, recent gender theorists have discerned a potentially subversive strategy in the idea that gender might be a mask rather than an essence. In her influential writings from the 1970s, the French feminist philosopher Luce Irigaray, for example, urges women to 'play with mimesis', to identify with the role of femininity 'without allowing [themselves] to be simply reduced to it'. Irigaray imagines that the 'playful repetition' of feminine traits would expose femininity as a performance, not a destiny (1985: 76). Irigaray's strategy of turning the womanly masquerade into a deliberate and parodic game has had a wide influence in gender theory. The theatre theorist Elin Diamond, for example, argues that feminists might adapt Brechtian ideas about acting to the performance of gender on stage and in everyday life. Diamond suggests that feminist theatre challenges the belief that gender is wholly natural by treating gender identity in much the same way that the actor in epic theatre relates to his or her character. Brechtian actors do not embody their characters, but offer a running commentary on them. For Diamond, feminist playwrights and performers defamiliarize gender roles by treating the conventional 'appearance, words, gestures, ideas, attitudes that constitute the gender lexicon' as merely 'illusionistic trappings', products of history, economics and power rather than nature (1997: 47).

The most important theorist to follow up on Irigaray's idea is Judith Butler, whose writings have had an important influence on contemporary theorists of gender and sexuality. In an essay entitled 'Imitation and Gender Insubordination' (1991), Butler argues that gender and sexual identity are forms of imitation without an original. Butler begins by noting that gays and lesbians have long been described as copies of heterosexual norms. Gay men are popularly depicted as effeminate 'queens', while lesbians are regarded as 'mannish' or 'butch'. Heterosexuality in these terms becomes a Platonic form, the would-be 'original' of which any other sexual identity is a defective imitation. For Butler, however, these familiar characterizations of gays and lesbians in fact describe the workings of all gender and sexual identity. She points to the example of drag performance, in which men parodically dress as women or women as men. Drag is an ostentatious example of the way all genders 'are appropriated, theatricalized, worn, and done' (Butler, 1991: 21). Like the drag performer, we all dress up as men or women every morning. Rather than being an aberrant exception, drag highlights the kind of performance we are expected to undertake whenever we appear before others and to repeat throughout our lives. The constructed quality of gender identity explains in large part the panicked reaction of homophobia. The homosexual 'imitation' reminds the heterosexual 'original' of its own constructedness. For this reason, Butler follows Irigaray in calling for a parodic mimicry of gender norms that highlights the artificiality of identity: 'The more the "act" is expropriated, the more the heterosexual claim to originality is exposed as illusory' (Butler, 1991: 23).

Butler argues that, although it bears all the marks of theatricality, gender performance is distinct on a number of levels. To begin with, gender is not something one freely chooses to perform. 'There is', Butler writes, 'no volitional subject behind the mime who decides, as it were, which gender it will be today' (1991: 24). Gender identity comes off the rack, for we can embody different styles of masculinity or femininity, but we are not free to choose our gender or sexuality, nor can we choose to be no gender at all. One is simply not comprehensible to others apart from his or her relationship to gender. Echoing Erving Goffman's account of selfhood as a 'peg' on which constructed roles are hung for a time – which we discussed in chapter 4 – Butler further argues that gender performances in fact produce the original subject who is said to act them out. Rather than being the visible expression of some internal and essential original, gender identity is a collection of imitated gestures and styles that come to seem natural. There is nothing authentically feminine about long hair or painted fingernails. Rather, through their compulsory imitation, these traits produce what Roland Barthes called a 'reality effect', which derives the appearance of nature out of the repetition of conventions. Gender is an 'imitation that produces the very notion of the original as an *effect* and consequence of the imitation itself' (Butler, 1991: 21). It is a form of what Butler calls 'psychic mimesis', a melancholic introjection of norms that we come to 'wear' on our skin, or embody in the 'array of corporeal theatrics' that define gender identity (Butler, 1991: 28). In this sense, we are all like the child in Freud's example who 'became' the kitten he lost. Gender is an impossible ideal that structures the core of our being and the appearance of our bodies through the process of identification.

Theorists of race and imperialism have offered a similar but distinct analysis of the mimetic foundations of identity. The pivotal figure here is the psychoanalyst and anti-colonial theorist Frantz Fanon. In his book, *Black Skin, White Masks* (1952), Fanon explores the formation of racial identity in the context of colonial domination. His specific point of reference is the psychic state of blacks in the French Antilles. Drawing on the Freudian theory of identification, Fanon argues that the colonial relationship is metaphorically akin to that between parent and child: the native is a 'child' in relation to the 'mother country'. Colonial subjects thus model themselves on the white colonists:

> there is a constellation of postulates, a series of propositions that slowly and subtly – with the help of books, newspapers, schools and their texts, advertisements, films, radio – work their way into one's mind and shape one's view of the world of the group to which one belongs.
>
> (Fanon, 1967: 152)

Because they have formed themselves according to the 'postulates' of another race, the colonial subject is psychically white and 'does not altogether apprehend the fact of his being a Negro' (Fanon, 1967: 162).

Fanon offers the example of a black child who reads about white explorers in his school books. This child 'identifies himself with the explorer, the bringer of civilization, the white man who carries truth to the savages', that is, with the very figures who oppress his people (Fanon, 1967: 147).

Over time, 'the young Negro subjectively adopts a white man's attitude' (Fanon, 1967: 147), and soon becomes 'a complete replica of the white man', at least in his own mind (Fanon, 1967: 36). But there is a tragic gap between the child's identifications and the political world he or she occupies. The black colonial subject who visits the predominantly white mother country, for example, is immediately defined as other. 'Overnight', Fanon writes, 'the Negro has been given two frames of reference within which he has to place himself' (1967: 110). By way of his identifications, he is psychically white. But because his skin is black, he is treated as essentially different from, and inherently inferior to, whites. Fanon gives the example of his own 'identification' as black by a white child. When this child points to him and cries 'Look, a Negro', Fanon realizes that 'I was an object in the midst of other objects' (1967: 109). Entirely defined by his skin colour, Fanon is denied status as a person. As Fuss has suggested, Fanon here underscores the cruel 'double command' that the colonial subject is called upon to obey: 'be like me, don't be like me; be mimetically identical, be totally other' (Fuss, 1995: 146). The conflict between internalized (or as Fanon calls it, 'epidermalized') identifications and external appearance generates a split identity for any racial minority. No matter how much the black child tries to imitate whites, he or she will always be marked as other.

In his influential development of Fanon's analysis, the contemporary post-colonial theorist Homi Bhabha casts the predicament of the colonized subject explicitly in terms of mimesis. Bhabha explores this predicament from the perspective of both the colonizer and the colonized. The colonizer, he argues, in his essay 'Of Mimicry and Man' (1987), reads the colonial other according to the Platonic paradigm: the natives must seem enough like the colonizers to be comprehensible and reformable, but different enough to justify their subordination to a foreign power. The colonial subject is thus cast as a poor imitation of the European original: 'colonial mimicry is the desire for a reformed, recognizable Other, *as a subject of a difference that is almost the same but not quite*' (Bhabha, 1994: 86). Colonial discourse turns the problematic status of the copy in Plato's theory into a source of political authority. The colonized subjects are, as Fanon noted, repeatedly encouraged to identify with the mother country. They are trained in its educational system, encouraged to adopt its manners, and converted by its missionaries. But for the colonizer, this identification necessarily and deliberately fails: 'in order to be effective, mimicry must continually produce its slippage, its excess, its difference' (Bhabha, 1994: 86). This difference reveals the colonial subject to be a 'mere' imitation, and posits the colonist as an original. Mimicry produces 'an authorized version of otherness' not to be confused with the real thing (Bhabha, 1994: 88).

Fuss notes that, despite a number of surface similarities, Bhabha's account of colonial mimicry entails a significantly different version of mimesis than we find in Irigaray and Butler. Much as, for Butler, the depiction of homosexuality as a bad copy transforms heterosexuality into an unproblematic original, so Bhabha sees mimesis as a tool for justifying colonial domination by setting the colonial subject up as a mere imitation. But in contrast with gender theorists, who regard mimesis as a potentially subversive strategy for challenging the fixity of gender identity, Bhabha argues that racial mimicry is 'one of the most elusive and effective strategies of colonial power and knowledge' (1994: 85). Although he allows for the possibility that racial mimicry might have some of the same effects that Butler discerns in drag, mimesis in the colonial context remains an express order given by the rulers to the subjugated, not the naturalized belief of the majority. Racial mimicry, therefore, is less susceptible to parody and alienation effects. The colonial subjects, Fuss writes of Bhabha's formulation, 'are constrained to impersonate the image the colonizer offers them of themselves; they are commanded to imitate the colonizer's version of their essential difference' (Fuss, 1995: 146). One person's subversion, in short, is another person's subjugation. This does not mean that the practice of gender mimicry that both Irigaray and Butler promote is doomed to failure, nor that colonial mimicry is an inescapable prison, only that the subversive as well as the subjugating effects of mimesis are a matter of context and interpretation, not something inherent to the performance itself.

Fuss highlights what Freud called the ambivalence of identification, its ability to bring about both love and hostility, both subversion and control. As we have seen, this ambivalence has attended discussions of mimesis from Plato to the present. Plato described mimesis as a drug: in the wrong hands, what cures can also harm. Of course, this insight is no secret even to the youngest school children, who mimic both to praise (say, an admired celebrity) and to deride (a hated teacher or peer). More powerfully, however, identification carries the theory of mimesis far beyond questions of art and theatre, insisting upon the 'fundamental mimetology', as Lacoue-Labarthe terms it, of human identity. Although identity may be shaped by our parents, and circumscribed by social and political forces, Freud's theory also implies, very much in line with Plato's account of childhood development, that it can potentially be fashioned according to any pattern one wants to give it.

7

MIMESIS AND CULTURE

SYMPATHETIC MAGIC

The concept of identification was only one important version of mimesis to arise out of the late nineteenth-century renewal of interest in this ancient problem. Like Freud and other psychologists, sociologists and anthropologists also looked to imitation as a way of understanding human social and cultural life. The theory of mimesis helped social theorists to explain the origins of language, the nature of groups and the transmission of culture over the generations. As early as the mid-eighteenth century, Jean-Jacques Rousseau, whose theory of acting we discussed in chapter 4, asserted that mimesis lies at the very foundation of human social life. For Rousseau, as for Plato, imitation is at once necessary and deceptive, a way of pretending to be what we are not, and a cause of dangerous and unreasonable emotions. In his influential work of educational theory, *Emile* (1762), Rousseau follows Plato and Aristotle in suggesting that mimesis is an integral part of human nature, but he also argues that this faculty is perverted in society by envy and vanity:

> Man is an imitator. Even animals are. The taste for imitation belongs to well-ordered nature, but in society it degenerates into vice. The ape imitates man whom he fears and does not imitate the animals whom he despises. He judges to be good what is done by a being better than he.
>
> (Rousseau, 1979: 104)

Prior to the formation of societies, according to Rousseau, human beings lived entirely within themselves. Once they became part of a collective, however, they began to look at others, and to want others to look at them. Henceforth, people would imitate not to learn or to improve themselves, but 'to make an impression on others', or to bring what is better down to their own level. 'The foundation of imitation among us', he concludes, 'comes from the desire always to be transported out of ourselves' (Rousseau, 1979: 104). Imitation is at once a primary social bond and a weak link in human nature that undermines individuality and makes us no better than apes.

Rousseau's account of imitation stresses conscious acts of mimesis in social life, but other nineteenth-century social theorists anticipated Freud in pointing out unwitting or unconscious forms of mimesis in culture. Karl Marx, for example, uses the traditional imagery of mimesis to highlight the ways in which the products of human thought and labour gain an independent and seemingly natural life of their own, a process he calls ideology. In a classic statement of this idea, in *The German Ideology* (1846), Marx draws upon an image of technological mimesis: 'If in all ideology men and their circumstances appear upside-down as in a *camera obscura*, this phenomenon arises just as much from their historical life-process as the inversion of objects on the retina does from their physical life-process' (Marx, 1978: 154). A camera obscura is a darkened chamber with a small aperture through which light reflected from objects outside projects an image on the opposite surface of the chamber. As with the negative in a modern film camera or, to use Marx's second metaphor, the surface of the retina, the image projected in the camera obscura is inverted. For Marx, ideology inverts the actual nature of human life-processes, creating the illusion that governments, economic systems or philosophical theories are eternal and inevitable rather than the result of human actions and choices.

Through this process, people are persuaded to subject themselves to laws and hierarchies they have the power to change. As the French philosopher Sarah Kofman has noted, Marx's image of the camera obscura rewrites Plato's allegory of the cave, which we discussed in chapter 1. Inside the camera obscura is the illusion, while outside is reality (Kofman, 1999: 14). For Marx, however, the real is not, as for Plato, rational forms, but the actual life-processes of human beings.

As these examples suggest, the accounts of social mimesis in both Rousseau and Marx remain within the Platonic tradition of treating mimesis as a source of deception and a false representation of reality. By the end of the nineteenth century, however, imperialism and the increasing globalization of trade, along with improved methods for international travel, brought Western intellectuals into closer contact with a wide variety of foreign and pre-modern cultures, whose ideas about and practices of imitation offered a disorienting challenge to the Platonic paradigm. One of the central areas of interest among social theorists, in this regard, was magic. According to the influential British anthropologist Sir James Frazer, who was among the first systematically to describe the concept, the major forms of magic are all governed by a theory of 'sympathy'. Magical practices, Frazer argues in his classic work *The Golden Bough* (1890), assume that 'things act on each other at a distance through a secret sympathy' (1922: 14). This sympathetic network binds humans, animals and objects in a kind of mimetic network of reciprocal influence. Frazer dismisses magic as a 'spurious system of natural law as well as a fallacious guide of conduct', and suggests that modern science has rendered it a mere relic of the 'primitive' past: what pre-modern cultures superstitiously attribute to mimesis, science understands in terms of laws (1922: 13). His account of its operation would nevertheless have a profound, if indirect, impact on the theory of mimesis in the twentieth century.

Frazer divides the workings of sympathetic magic into two basic principles. The first principle, which he terms the Law of Similarity, suggests that like produces like, or that an effect resembles its cause. This is the logic of 'imitative magic', in which 'the magician infers that he can produce any effect he desires merely by imitating it' (Frazer, 1922: 12). He might seek to injure an enemy by destroying an image of him, mime the behaviour of an animal tribal hunters want to catch, or 'annul an evil omen by accomplishing it in mimicry' (Frazer, 1922: 42). The second principle, which Frazer calls the Law of Contact, suggests that things that have once been in contact continue to act on each other at a distance. This principle underlies 'contagious magic', in which the magician uses body parts or personal belongings to affect the person with whom they were once in contact. Although Frazer treats these laws as structurally distinct, the French anthropologists Marcel Mauss and Henri Hubert argue, in *A General Theory of Magic* (1902), that the principles of imitation and contact merge in practice. Magic based on imitation typically involves contact: the magician will often manipulate the magical copy, or wave a magic wand. By the same token, magic based on contact implies a relationship of similarity between the substance and the person to whom it once belonged (Mauss, 1972: 72). Frazer himself gives the example of footprints, common objects of magical rites, which at once resemble a foot and are produced by contact (1922: 52), and also notes that charms used in imitative magic often incorporate the hair or nails of the intended victim (1922: 15).

Recent anthropologists have suggested that the entire category of magic is an artefact of European ethnocentrism, for which any unfamiliar forms of thought are defective or primitive rather than simply different. But Frazer's theory, particularly through its less dismissive and more systematic rethinking by Mauss and Hubert, was highly suggestive for intellectuals in the early twentieth century. The magical thinking Frazer dismissed as merely unscientific struck these intellectuals as a potentially radical new way of understanding mimesis. Indeed, like aspects of Freudian identification, the anthropological account of magic stretches the Platonic paradigm to its limits. Socrates refers to the imitator as a 'wizard' (Plato, 1991: 281), but the magician operates in a very different world from the one in which Plato's imitator does. Magical copies have real properties and genuine powers of their own. They belong to a network of reciprocal sympathies, not a hierarchical ladder of rational forms and material embodiments. Indeed, the anthropologist Michael Taussig argues that magic should 'make us reconsider our very notion of what it means to be an image of some thing' (1993: 57). In its practical confounding of similarity and contact, Taussig suggests, magic belies Plato's claim that images lack reality. Unlike the Platonic copy, the magical copy is made of the same stuff as the original.

It is a new configuration of matter, and not an immaterial reflection of it. Similarly, the magical copy is a means of affecting the original. Magic does not rigorously distinguish between image and matter, the real and the imaginary. In magical mimesis, Taussig suggests, the copy draws on the character and power of the original to such an extent that 'the representation may even assume that character and that power' (1993: xiii).

MIMICRY AND THE MIMETIC FACULTY

Anthropological accounts of pre-modern imitation and sympathetic magic directly inform three important discussions of mimesis from the 1930s and 1940s: the German literary and social critic Walter Benjamin's theory of the 'mimetic faculty'; the French social theorist Roger Caillois' discussion of insect mimicry, which was a decisive influence on Lacan's theory of the mirror stage; and the German philosopher Theodor Adorno's account of the historical decline of mimesis under the influence of Western reason. Although none of these theorists makes magic central to his discussion of mimesis, each regards the workings of sympathetic magic as evidence of a foundational, even bio-physical, tendency toward imitation. Benjamin, Caillois and Adorno also write self-consciously in the wake of Marx, Nietzsche and Freud, for whom, as I have noted, modernity is not seen as the pinnacle of human development but as the alienated and self-deceptive issue of economic inequality and unconscious psychological forces. Magic, in this light, provides these three theorists with an incisive means of questioning the Platonic tradition. They all trace out a history of mimesis that begins well before Plato, and in which modernity is a repetition of archaic thought, not its overcoming. Indeed, rather than having freed itself of primitive mimetic thinking, as Frazer argues, modernity remains mimetic through and through, but is blind to, deceived about or neglectful of its mimetism.

In his posthumously published essay 'The Mimetic Faculty' (1933), Benjamin constructs a speculative history of mimesis itself, and not just of theories about it. Nature incessantly produces similarities, Benjamin argues. Human beings are the most mimetic of creatures, yet our current ability to discern and produce similarities is only 'a rudiment of the once powerful compulsion to become similar and to behave mimetically' (Benjamin, 1978: 333). What was in pre-modern cultures an all-encompassing drive to imitate and to find similarities in the world is now reduced to rational processes such as discerning the similarity between copy and original. But this does not mean that mimesis has entirely disappeared from modernity. 'The question', Benjamin asks, 'is whether we are concerned with the decay of this faculty or with its transformation' (1978: 334). Many aspects of modern life suggest a decay of mimesis. Children's play, for example, 'is everywhere permeated by mimetic modes of behavior' (Benjamin, 1978: 333). Children imitate everything, from adult occupations to windmills and trains, but give up this rich mimetic world when they become adults. Benjamin finds much the same narrowing of the mimetic faculty on the level of human history: 'the sphere of life that formerly seemed to be governed by the law of similarity was comprehensive; it ruled both microcosm and macrocosm' (1978: 333). He points to 'magical correspondences and analogies that were familiar to ancient peoples' (Benjamin, 1978: 334). Astrology, for example, imagined a mimetic bond linking each life to the position of the stars.

Children's play, sympathetic magic and astrology are all instances of what Benjamin calls 'nonsensuous similarity'. This term describes similarities not just between things that materially resemble one another but between the animate and inanimate, the microcosm and the macrocosm. The child's imitation of a windmill is based on nonsensuous similarity, as is the tendency of ancient cultures to find clues to human character in the stars. Although we no longer encounter nonsensuous similarities in every corner of creation, Benjamin asserts that we still produce them, and thus continue to rely on the mimetic faculty, albeit one greatly transformed. The crucial means for the formation of nonsensuous similarities in modernity is language. Language itself, Benjamin argues, is fundamentally mimetic. Onomatopoeia (a word that imitates a sound, like saying 'clang' for the sound of a bell) is the most obvious instance of linguistic mimesis, but Benjamin has something more thoroughgoing in mind. The possibility of translation, for example, suggests that different words in different languages bear a nonsensuous similarity to a common concept. The words are similar, even though they do not resemble each other. Written language, likewise, is 'an archive of nonsensuous similarities, of nonsensuous correspondences' between sound and script, and between text and world (Benjamin, 1978: 335). The act of reading allows us to imagine things that extend far beyond the black marks on the page. Like the ancient prophet reading entrails, the modern reader of a novel discerns similarities that fuse the material medium of language with a 'flash' of similarity (Benjamin, 1978: 335). Letters look no more like the scenes we imagine than entrails resemble the fate of a people. But both forms of reading suggest that the mimetic faculty continues to operate even in activities that seem wholly non-mimetic.

For Benjamin, the nonsensuous similarities in language have absorbed earlier forms of mimesis, and thereby 'liquidated' magic and astrology for modern cultures (1978: 336). Modernity is at once less mimetic than and differently mimetic from antiquity. Caillois, by contrast, regards mimesis as a perennial instinct of all life forms, one that does not essentially differ in insects and in humans. In 'Mimicry and Legendary Psychasthenia' (1935), he seeks to explain the strange fact that many insect species have evolved to mimic their surroundings. Although most studies of this phenomenon see mimicry as an offensive or defensive adaptation, a way of surprising prey or tricking predators, Caillois approaches it as part of a more primal relationship between the organism and its surroundings. As Caillois notes, some examples of mimicry lack obvious advantages for survival. Many of the predators from whom mimetic insects try to hide hunt by smell and not by sight, so visual mimicry does not provide much protection from them. Other mimetic adaptations do not seem to be functional at all. Some mimetic species are inedible and therefore have nothing to fear from predators. In other cases mimesis is even suicidal, as with certain insects that forage among the leaves they imitate and can mistakenly eat others of their own species.

Such examples lead Caillois to question the evolutionary account of mimicry. Rather than being a useful adaptation, insect mimesis is a biological 'luxury'. Caillois compares it with sympathetic magic, which epitomizes the 'overwhelming tendency to imitate, combined with a belief in the efficacy of this imitation', that marks both 'primitive' and 'civilized' humanity. Insect mimicry, he suggests, is akin to '*an incantation fixed at its culminating point* and having caught the sorcerer in his own trap' (Caillois, 1984: 27). Both the mimetic insect and imitative magic embody a universal mimetic drive that exceeds considerations of usefulness or self-preservation. Caillois discerns in all forms of mimesis 'a disturbance in the perception of space' (1984: 28). In adapting itself to its surroundings, the imitator is also depersonalized, becoming just one point in space among others. 'He is similar', Caillois writes, 'not similar to something, but just *similar*'. Caillois finds in this spatial depersonalization a key to understanding mental illness, which he calls 'psychasthenia'. 'This assimilation to space', he argues, 'is necessarily accompanied by a decline in the feeling of personality and life' (Caillois, 1984: 30). The personality becomes less distinct, less marked off from its surroundings, and is thus rendered permeable to other influences. Mimicry thus inverts Lacan's mirror stage, where the ego sets itself off from its surroundings by distinguishing the inner world from the image. For Caillois, biological and magical imitation point more broadly to an 'instinct of renunciation' that, contrary to the instinct of self-preservation, orients the organism 'toward a reduced existence, which in the end would no longer know either consciousness or feeling' (1984: 32). Somewhat like what Freud called the 'death drive', mimesis draws the organism back to the inorganic state, into an undifferentiated relationship to the environment.

Both Benjamin and Caillois argue that mimesis is historically and developmentally significant, and both theorists find evidence of a mimetic faculty in modernity. They differ, however, on the question of whether mimesis itself changes over time. For Benjamin, the mimetic faculty is mutable, altering to accommodate new conditions. For Caillois, by contrast, mimesis is a nearly universal biological drive. In his book *Man, Play, and Games* (1958), for example, he compares the way spectators unconsciously move in imitation of athletes they are watching to the choreographed motion of insect swarms (Caillois, 1961: 22). Given the charged political context of 1930s, marked by worldwide economic depression and the rise of fascism in Europe, it is not difficult to read a political subtext into both of these accounts of mimesis. Mimesis becomes a way of explaining the seemingly irrational elements of modernity, from mass political movements, where followers wear the same outfits and share the same hatreds, to economic panics, in which investors make suicidal financial decisions in imitation of others and not for their own good.

Politicizing mimesis is the explicit project of *The Dialectic of Enlightenment* (1946), by the German philosophers and social critics Max Horkheimer and Theodor Adorno. Written during the Second World War, *The Dialectic of Enlightenment* is an ambitious effort to question the entire Western conception of reason, a conception that seemed to allow, and perhaps even fostered, fascism and the concentration camps. Adorno, who wrote the book's theoretical account of mimesis, explicitly draws on and brings out the political implication of the theories proposed by Benjamin and Caillois, as well as Freud's notion of identification, in order to explain the decay of mimesis in modernity. For Adorno, the term Enlightenment refers both to the idealization of rationality and science in eighteenth-century and modern thought and to a longer tradition in Western philosophy of privileging abstract reason over the senses and emotion. Adorno argues that this tradition violently distances the self from nature, and subjects the outer world of things and the inner world of thought to the totalitarian administration of the isolated individual. Against this tendency, Adorno reimagines the act of knowing as physical and mimetic rather than methodical. Mimesis is the repressed underside of the Enlightenment, the 'biological prehistory' of humanity from which reason arises, but which rational thought rejects (Horkheimer and Adorno, 1972: 180). Whereas Frazer sees science as an overcoming of mimetic superstitions, Adorno argues that the scientific sprit has violently repressed potentially valuable mimetic ways of knowing, and thus narrowed the range of human knowing.

Adorno defines mimesis as the way an organism adapts itself to its environment. Following Caillois, he suggests that it is not originally a conscious act of imitation, but a physiological response to danger. When the body freezes out of fear it becomes like 'circumambient, motionless nature'. 'Protection as fear', he writes, 'is a form of mimicry' (Horkheimer and Adorno, 1972: 180). To this extent, mimesis is a primordial form of rationality, a means of reacting to the external world. Where Enlightenment rationality seeks to standardize and classify, mimesis does not respect rigid divisions between subject and object. It is thus akin to 'touch, soothing, snuggling up, coaxing' (Horkheimer and Adorno, 1972: 182). Adorno also compares mimesis to the sense of smell. Unlike the more 'rational' sense of sight, which functions best at a distance from the object, smell literally mingles self and other. 'When we see', he writes, 'we remain what we are; but when we smell, we are taken over by otherness' (Horkheimer and Adorno, 1972: 184). In sum, rather than setting the world at a distance, mimesis brings it closer, and in place of the hierarchical Platonic opposition between copy and original, mimesis forges a bridge between self and other. Because mimesis threatens the autonomy of the isolated ego, reason tries to overcome it. 'Civilization has replaced the organic adaptation to others and mimetic behavior proper', Adorno writes, 'by organized control of mimesis, in the magical phase; and finally, by rational practice, by work, in the historical phase' (Horkheimer and Adorno, 1972: 180). The history of Western rationality entails the systematic repression of mimesis. Magic turns mimesis into an instrument, making resemblances a means of affecting the world, and work turns human beings into instruments, replacing the mimetic faculty with the empty repetitions of factory labour. As for both Benjamin and Caillois, for Adorno mimesis does not disappear from human life. Instead, it lives on as the repressed and mutilated other of modernity, in the identical uniforms and repeated chants of fascist mobs, and in the quasi-magical power commodities have over our desires.

MIMETIC DESIRE: GIRARD

Although Plato is not central to their history of mimesis, Horkheimer and Adorno implicitly situate him at the origin of modernity. Rather than inaugurating the mimetic tradition, Plato marks its end. Mimesis, for Plato, as for the Enlightenment rationality he inaugurates, is an obstacle to philosophical knowledge, not a distinct means of knowing the world and the other. We find a very similar historical repositioning of Plato, although towards a very different account of mimesis, in the influential work of the French literary and cultural theorist René Girard. Like Benjamin, Caillois and Adorno, Girard regards mimesis as a primordial tendency in human life, one which, he argues, Plato profoundly misinterprets. 'If Plato distrusts art', Girard writes, 'it is because art is a form of mimesis, and not the reverse' (1987: 15). Plato's overwhelming influence has, he argues, led subsequent theorists to reduce the field of mimesis to art and images rather than to study the mimetic nature of human action more generally. For Girard, mimesis is a dynamic social force that lies at the origins of religion and culture. But whereas Adorno argues that the control of mimesis underlies the development of rationalistic modernity, Girard suggests that uncontrolled mimesis threatens social stability. Mimesis is not the utopian other of reason, but the origin of violence and conflict.

Girard first finds evidence of what he calls mimetic desire not in philosophy or sociology but in the history of the novel. In his important study *Deceit, Desire, and the Novel* (1961), Girard uses this history to question the prevailing Romantic myth that regards desire as spontaneous, original and unique to each individual. He argues instead for a theory of desire as mimetic and conflictual. Rather than desiring an object directly, out of some perceived need or in the service of a moral imperative, the heroes of novels, Girard notes, often desire in imitation of a third party, whom Girard calls a mediator. The basic structure of desire is triangular. The object is at the apex of the triangle, while the subject and the mediator form two points at the base. Desire is socially oriented: we always desire what others desire, in imitation of them, and not on our own impetus. Our desires are second hand, never properly ours from the start: 'the mediator himself desires the object, or could desire it: it is even this very desire, real or presumed, which makes this object infinitely desirable in the eyes of the subject' (Girard, 1965: 7).

Girard insists that mimetic desire should not be reduced to the Platonic paradigm. Although always imitated, desire cannot be divided into original and copy, the ideal form and its pale reflection. Instead, deriving a broad anthropological theory from his literary examples, Girard posits the existence of 'a desiring mimesis prior to all representation and all selection of object' (1978: 89). Once our basic needs are satisfied, we still possess an undefined reservoir of desire not bound to an object. This desire is given direction by the mediator who appears to desire originally and autonomously, and thus becomes a role model. But the mediator's autonomy is an illusion, for there are no originals when it comes to desire. Originality is an effect of desire, not its truth. While the child happily imitates others, 'the adult likes to assert his independence and to offer himself as a model for others' (Girard, 1977: 146). Adults imagine that their own desire, like that of the mediator, is original, but one person's master is another person's disciple. 'From all indications', he writes, 'only the disciple is truly essential – it is this role that must be invoked to define the basic human condition' (Girard, 1977: 147). Desire is passed from person to person in a chain of imitations that only look original to the deluded imitator.

In *Deceit, Desire, and the Novel*, Girard sketches out a structural model of mimetic desire based on this foundational insight. He identifies two categories of mediation: external and internal. In external mediation, the other is so distant, socially or historically, that the subject can openly avow his or her imitation. Girard associates this kind of mediation with the practice of *imitatio*, and in particular, with Don Quixote, who becomes a knight in conscious imitation of the fictional knights in chivalric romances. In instances of internal mediation, by contrast, the mediator is close enough to become a rival. 'Internal mediation is present', Girard writes, 'when one "catches" a nearby desire just as one would catch the plague or cholera, simply by contact with an infected person' (1965: 99). Girard's key example is jealousy in the novels of Stendhal and the twentieth-century French novelist Marcel Proust. Jealousy, for these writers, is always triangular. Heroes become jealous when the object of their desire is desired by another, whether this rival desire is genuine or imaginary. Modern advertising provides ready examples of both forms of mediation. Advertisers rely on external mediation when they pay celebrities to use a product, and make use of internal mediation when they depict common people using common products. In the first case, they want our admiration for the celebrity to spark a desire for the product, and in the second case, they want us to 'catch' the nearby desire of someone like ourselves.

Both external and internal mediation demonstrate that desire is produced by mimesis, not need. We desire not because the object is necessary to us, but because someone else wants it. While external mediation is relatively stable, internal mediation, Girard argues, can lead to violence and conflict. Willing disciples or political subordinates recognize their distance from the master, but the internal mediator seems to have no stronger claim to the object than does the subject of desire. The social and political equality between subject and mediator inevitably leads to conflict: 'desire always increases in intensity as the mediator approaches the desiring subject' (Girard, 1965: 83). This conflict can also become reciprocal, leading to a phenomenon Girard calls 'double mediation', in which the mediator imitates the desire of his or her own imitator. The mediator here is 'tempted to copy the copy of his own desire' (Girard, 1965: 99). Double mediation leads to a kind of mimetic feedback loop, so that, by contrast with the Platonic paradigm, the object itself becomes a matter of indifference. 'In double mediation', Girard writes, 'it is not that one wants the object, but that one does not want to see it in someone else's hands' (1965: 102). Although it takes the form of a struggle for an object, double mediation is really a struggle between mutual imitators. It is, to this extent, 'a veritable "generator" of desire, the simplest possible' (Girard, 1965: 173). Sexual jealousy is the paradigm for double mediation, but Girardian scholars have also noted its workings in phenomena such as speculative bubbles, during which investors become so fearful of missing out on potential profits that they pay exorbitant amounts of money for commodities of dubious value, such as tulip bulbs or technology stocks. In speculative bubbles, investors respond to the desire of other investors, to the fear of not having what someone else might have, and not to the inherent value of the objects they are buying.

In a series of books from the 1970s and 1980s, Girard applies the theory of mimetic desire to a wide range of cultural phenomena, as well as finding evidence of mimetic conflict in literary texts drawn from nearly every period of Western history. 'If human beings suddenly ceased imitating', he claims, 'all forms of culture would vanish' (Girard, 1987: 7). Imitative desire is common to human and animals, and originates in a basic tendency towards appropriation and domination that Girard calls 'acquisitive mimesis'. 'When any gesture of appropriation is imitated', Girard writes, 'it simply means that two hands will reach for the same object simultaneously: conflict cannot fail to result' (1978: 201). Mimetic desire invites rivalry, and rivalry leads to conflict and strife. Violence is an effect of double mediation, resulting 'when two or more partners try to prevent one another from appropriating the object they all desire' (Girard, 1979: 9). Many human institutions are designed to control the threat of 'runaway mimesis', the spiral of violence that can arise out of the structure of double mediation. This is true of taboos, which forbid certain mimetic behaviours, and of modern judicial systems, which replace the mimetic 'eye-for-an-eye' cycle of revenge with an objective mediator (the judge and jury) and fixed penalties.

The linchpin in this system of control is sacrifice. In ritual sacrifice, the community redirects the violence produced by mimetic rivalries onto a surrogate victim. The phenomenon of scapegoating is exemplary of this redirection. The scapegoat takes on the violence of the community, transforming mimetic desire into a source of social stability. 'Mimesis', Girard notes, 'is mimetically attractive' and can spread from the initial subject and mediator to an entire community (1979: 12). This mimesis of mimesis underlies the formation of mobs, which are marked by uncannily uniform behaviour. Killing or expelling a scapegoat satisfies the mob by substituting a common enemy for a common object of desire, in effect reversing the flow of mimesis. Instead of being divided by acquisitive mimesis, the members of the mob are united by what Girard calls 'conflictual mimesis', which replaces desire for the object with hatred toward it (1987: 26). Sacrificing the scapegoat effects a catharsis of mimesis in the community. The tragic catharsis that Aristotle identifies is but a particular instance of this more fundamental social process (Girard, 1977: 291). The scapegoat effect also explains, for Girard, the crucial difference of Christianity from other religions. All other religions, he argues, produce stability through ritual sacrifice, but the Bible alone takes the perspective of the victim. Christ is divinely innocent, and his sufferings at the hands of a mob are depicted as unjust. The Bible thus reveals the mimetic forces that sacrificial religions only redirect rather than eliminate. Historically, Girard argues, this lesson has been misunderstood, since scapegoating is no less prevalent in Christian communities than in any other. In essence, however, '[f]ollowing Christ means giving up mimetic desire', along with the cycle of violence it produces and sacrificial means of deflecting it (Girard, 1987: 431).

Many of Girard's readings of literary texts concern the failure of Western culture to understand this lesson. In *Deceit, Desire, and the Novel*, for example, he notes that all of the great novels about mimesis end with a 'conversion', in which the hero, like Christ, renounces mimetic desire as a dangerous illusion. Rather than pointing to the hero's failure, such renunciations suggest that writers such as Stendhal and Proust understood the mechanism of mimetic desire far better than Plato and Aristotle did. Girard finds evidence of this understanding in Shakespeare as well. In a reading of *Hamlet* included in his book

A Theater of Envy (1991), Girard argues that one of the most familiar critical questions about the play, namely why Hamlet delays in taking revenge on Claudius, is fundamentally misguided. Although *Hamlet* is written in the traditional form of revenge tragedy, which was to Elizabethan theatre what thrillers are to contemporary film, Shakespeare in fact uses the form to express a deep suspicion about the mimetic logic of revenge. Hamlet, Girard argues, feels a 'weariness with revenge' (1991: 273), and his delay is an effort to overcome the sense that taking vengeance would only make him into the mimetic double of Claudius: the murderer of a king. For Girard, Hamlet does not lack courage, but he is unwilling to participate in the cycle of violence that led to the murder of his father. The rottenness in the state of Denmark is uncontrolled mimesis, not just the individuals who embody it. The fact that *Hamlet* remains such a fascinating play for students and scholars is, for Girard, evidence that it touches upon our own refusal to renounce mimetic desire and the logic of sacrifice, and thus offers 'a powerful intimation of what the modern world is really about' (1991: 284).

SIMULACRA AND HYPERREALITY

All of the anthropological theories we have discussed in this chapter consider the workings of mimesis in human behaviours and cultural phenomena beyond or prior to the beginnings of mimetic art. They criticize Plato for restricting his account of mimesis to painting and poetry, and suggest that his thinking on the subject is too narrow or no longer wholly relevant. But for an important group of French intellectuals in the 1960s and 1970s, the Platonic paradigm is not so easily dismissed. This paradigm, they argue, is so integral to Western thought that the only way out of Platonism is through Plato himself. This is the argument of two important essays from the late 1960s and the early 1970s, by the French philosophers Gilles Deleuze and Jacques Derrida respectively. Platonic theory and the long tradition it has inspired, both philosophers argue, render mimesis merely the shadowy other of truth that only illustrates or reflects something real. But Deleuze and Derrida find cracks in the Platonic edifice and use Plato's own formulations to discern the paradoxical possibility of a copy not bound to a true or singular original.

In 'Plato and the Simulacrum' (1967), Deleuze argues that Plato in fact describes two forms of imitation in his various accounts of mimesis. On the one hand, there are copies, which are 'well-founded pretenders, guaranteed by resemblance' (Deleuze, 1990: 257). On the other hand, there are simulacra, which look like copies but differ from the original in crucial respects. In his dialogue the *Sophist,* Plato names these two 'species' of image *eikastic* and *phantastic. Eikastic* images (or copies) are exact replicas, which conform to the size, proportions and colour of the original. *Phantastic* images (or simulacra) correct their proportions to account for the position of the viewer. A very large work, for example, could not reproduce the model in every detail, since 'the upper parts would look too small, and the lower too large, because we see one at a distance, the other close at hand' (Plato, 1989: 978). *Phantastic* images distort their physical form, diverging from the exact details of the original to correct for the limitations of vision. This is the case with many statues designed for Greek temples, which would not be viewed at eye level, and compensated for the position of the spectator. Copies are somewhat like the carpenter's material couch in the *Republic*, and so are acceptable imitations for Plato; simulacra, however, only appear to resemble the original from a specific point of view, and are therefore suspect. 'The copy', Deleuze writes, 'is an image endowed with resemblance, the simulacrum is an image without resemblance' (1990: 257). The simulacrum copies only the appearance of the original.

For Deleuze, the distinction between copy and simulacrum has potentially profound implications. The simulacrum, he argues, is not an illegitimate distortion of the true original, as Plato insists, but an image that has broken free from any single original. It appeals to the contingent and historically grounded condition of the viewer, not to an abstract and purely rational conception of truth. Deleuze points to the example of pop art, a movement from the 1960s that took inspiration from popular and commercial culture. Andy Warhol's famous painting of a Campbell's soup can, to take an important instance of this style, has nothing to do with soup or canning. Instead, it treats the can as an image with a life of its own apart from its original. The millions of soup cans on supermarket shelves are copies; the soup can in Warhol's painting is a simulacrum. The simulacrum denies the hierarchy of copy and original, and thus becomes a potent rival to the

Platonic theory of mimesis. Warhol's soup can exists in the world on its own terms; it is an imitation, but it does not depend upon a material original (soup and tin) for its effect. Deleuze contrasts the simulacrum, in this regard, with the fake or the artificial, which still rely on the order of mimesis. Pirated books or movies, for example, want to be confused with the original, for their value derives from precisely this confusion. Thus the fake depends on our naive Platonism rather than questioning it. The simulacrum, by contrast, is a real thing in itself, not the good or bad imitation of something else. Accordingly, Deleuze declares, we should allow the simulacra to 'rise and affirm their rights among icons and copies' (1990: 262).

For Deleuze, modernity 'is defined by the power of the simulacrum', by the free circulation of images without truth (1990: 265). In his essay, 'The Double Session' (1970), Derrida bears out this observation by demonstrating how the nineteenth-century French poet Stéphane Mallarmé produces a simulacrum of Platonic mimesis itself. Derrida focuses on a short prose text called 'Mimique' (1886). Less than a page long, this text recounts an improvisational performance by the mime Paul Margueritte, entitled *Pierrot Murderer of his Wife*. The act comprises a single scenario, with all the parts played by Margueritte himself: Pierrot murders his unfaithful wife by tying her to a bed and tickling her to death. This performance balances uneasily between copy and simulacrum. On the one hand, the mime mimes, acts out a scene described in advance. But on the other hand, the act is largely improvisational, follows no written script, and thus has no discernable original. Even though Mallarmé gestures toward the Platonic tradition by calling his text 'Mimique', the mime in fact 'imitates nothing' (Derrida, 1981: 194). Margueritte's act is 'confined to a perpetual allusion': it seems to refer to something prior, to some textual or conceptual original, but does so 'without breaking the ice or mirror' that would finally differentiate the copy from what it imitates (Mallarmé, 1982: 69).

As Derrida shows, moreover, Mallarmé's text is by no means simply the description of a performance. Mallarmé discusses a book written by Margueritte about the performance, not the performance itself. Rather than describing the 'original' mime show, Mallarmé describes a textual 'copy' of it. This copy of a copy itself has a strange status. To begin with, it uses words to describe what was a silent performance, so the performance precedes the written 'script', rather than coming after it. The book is prefaced by an author's note, in which Margueritte claims that he was inspired to perform *Pierrot Murderer of his Wife* in part by the praise of Mallarmé. Mallarmé's text, finally, incorporates what seems to be a quotation from Margueritte's book that does not come from the book. It is the simulacrum of a quotation. All of these textual twists and turns lead Derrida to the conclusion that 'Mimique' frustrates any effort to differentiate copies from originals. Neither the performance itself nor the book that follows it has the obvious status of a true 'original'. 'Mallarmé thus preserves the differential structure of mimicry or *mimesis*', Derrida writes, 'but without its Platonic or metaphysical interpretation, which implies that somewhere the being of something that *is*, is being imitated' (1981: 206). Rather than trying to deny the tradition of mimesis, though, the text posits a network of copies that do not lead back to a singular truth. For Derrida, Mallarmé's simulacrum of mimesis is the only way to challenge the Platonic paradigm without repeating its habits of mind. 'Any attempt to reverse mimetologism', he writes, 'or escape it in one fell swoop by leaping out of it *with both feet* would only amount to an inevitable and immediate fall back into its system' (Derrida, 1981: 207). Unveiling the 'truth' of mimesis would only imitate Plato's founding gesture of judging mimesis in terms of truth.

Deleuze and Derrida both tend to locate resistance to the Platonic paradigm in the high-cultural products of European modernism, but theorists have increasingly found similar effects in the proliferation of images engendered by postmodern media culture, as Deleuze's brief reference to pop art suggests. According to these theorists, we live in a world of simulacra. Postmodern societies are so saturated with images that we can no longer distinguish the original from the copy. In a sense, postmodernity has returned to the pre-modern condition of sympathetic magic that theorists such as Benjamin, Caillois and Adorno describe: mimesis is inextricably woven into the fabric of reality itself. One of the earliest versions of this claim is the French theorist Guy Debord's book *The Society of the Spectacle* (1967), a manifesto of the Situationist International, a revolutionary artistic and political movement highly critical of modern commodity culture that was active in the 1960s. Debord argues that nineteenth-century capitalism, based on the production of commodities, has been superseded by a new capitalism based on the production of images. Instead of making useful things, capitalism now builds and sells appearances. Its centre of gravity has moved from the factory to the advertisement, and from satisfying needs to satisfying desires. 'All that was once directly lived', Debord writes, 'has become mere representation' (1994: 12). Spectacular capitalism makes society a passive audience of commodity fetishists, which interacts with the world by consuming things rather than producing them. Quite unlike Deleuze and Derrida, though, Debord retains a faith in the real. Because the spectacle has rendered real human relations theatrical, political action should reject the world of simulacra rather than exploit it.

The most important recent theorist of the simulacrum, French media and cultural theorist Jean Baudrillard draws upon Deleuze as well as Debord in his account of what he calls postmodern 'hyperreality'. In *Simulacra and Simulations* (1981), Baudrillard describes a world in which the distinction between real and imaginary, copy and original, no longer holds. 'It is no longer a question', he writes, 'of imitation, nor duplication, nor even parody. It is rather a question of substituting signs of the real for the real' (Baudrillard, 1994: 2). Baudrillard's key category is simulation, a kind of operational simulacrum. To dissimulate, he notes, is to pretend not to have what you in fact have. This is the definition of mimesis for Plato. To simulate, by contrast, is to pretend to have what one does not have. Like the simulacrum, simulation fits uneasily within the Platonic paradigm. Baudrillard offers the example of a psychosomatic who produces the symptoms of a disease without in fact being sick. 'Is the simulator sick or not', he asks, 'given that he produces "true" symptoms?' (Baudrillard, 1994: 3). The simulator is not dissimulating health, since his symptoms are 'real', but these symptoms cannot be traced back to an origin in the body. They are neither true nor false, neither real nor imaginary. The simulation has the objective qualities of the real without being real; it is a second-order reality, and not the reflection of a sovereign truth.

Indeed, for Baudrillard, the postmodern always confounds reality and simulation. A simulated robbery, for example, is not objectively different from a real one: 'the gestures, the signs are the same as for a real robbery' (Baudrillard, 1994: 20). In the absence of any objective evidence of simulation, Baudrillard notes, the police would be forced to treat the simulated crime as real, and might even fire real bullets. Yet all crimes today are in some sense simulated, 'inscribed in the decoding and orchestration rituals of the media' (Baudrillard, 1994: 21). Real criminals take their cues from movies and television, which in turn obsessively fictionalize true crime stories. Rather than being copies or originals, real and fictional crime are both 'hyperreal'. This does not mean that crime has no consequences, only that we can no longer definitively sort out the real from the imaginary. Baudrillard also points to the example of Disneyland, which simulates and miniaturizes the 'real' America. This simulation is not the reflection of an actual America that exists outside the gates. Rather, 'Disneyland is presented as imaginary in order to make us believe that the rest is real', that the simulation stops at the gates of the 'magic kingdom' (Baudrillard, 1994: 12). But this promise of the real is never fulfilled. Indeed, our contemporary mania for collecting, nostalgia and historical preservation embodies a panicked effort to capture a reality that seems to reside only in the past. The lure of the authentic is an implicit acknowledgement that we live in a world of fakes and simulations, that the real is a vanishing quality needing the protection of a museum.

We began this chapter by looking at the influence that ethnographic studies of magic had upon twentieth-century theories of mimesis. Baudrillard tellingly returns to the anthropological context in his account of the hyperreal. He describes a decision by the Philippine government in the early 1970s to return a small group of the Tasaday people to their original home deep in the jungle. This tribe had escaped contact with the outside world for centuries until modern anthropologists discovered them and introduced them to modern life. The anthropological community, however, came to fear that its research was destroying the very qualities that had made the tribe worth studying in the first place. But this seemingly well-meaning effort to preserve the tribe, Baudrillard remarks, has not restored their original reality, only rendered them hyperreal: 'frozen, cryogenized, sterilized, protected *to death*, they have become referential simulacra, and science itself has become pure simulation' (1994: 8). For Baudrillard we are all 'simulacral Indians'. Western culture has come to regard itself ethnographically, endlessly lamenting the loss of some primal authenticity. 'It is thus very naive', Baudrillard remarks:

> to look for ethnology in the Savages or in some Third World – it is here, everywhere, in the metropolises, in the White community, in a world completely catalogued and analyzed, and then *artificially resurrected under the auspices of the real.*
>
> (1994: 8)

We might suggest that the theory of mimesis, with its abiding faith in truth and reality, is for Baudrillard precisely what magic was to Frazer: a curious relic of the past that lingers anachronistically in a vastly altered world.

CONCLUSION
Memetics

I have sought in this book to follow a series of pathways though the dense network of images, ideas and philosophical problems that makes up the Western theory of mimesis. Unlike many other theories in literary and cultural thought ('ideology' is a prominent example), mimesis lacks a dramatic history of changing meanings and radical redefinitions. This is not to say, of course, that the concept has failed to inform the work of numerous writers throughout the Western cultural tradition. Quite the contrary. As we have seen, poets and philosophers from Plato and Aristotle to Augustine, Petrarch, Shakespeare, Diderot, Eliot, Freud, Auerbach, Brecht and Butler have incorporated some aspect of or response to the theory of mimesis in their work. But the concept of mimesis itself has developed little over time. Almost every theory we have encountered in this book begins in the works of Plato and Aristotle, even if only to reject them. Indeed, even the idea of escaping from mimesis, so dominant in twentieth-century thought, is there from the very start. The writings of Plato and Aristotle, along with their influence on later theorists, produced what I have called, following the German scholars Gebauer and Wulf, a 'thematic complex'. Elements of this complex appear with different emphases in different historical periods, but the complex itself remains remarkably consistent in its essential contours. Some thematic elements of mimesis commonly appear together, others separately. But none of them is ever wholly out of reach.

Put in slightly different terms, we might suggest that the theory of mimesis, much like the 'big bang' for theorists of cosmology, did not simply inaugurate an intellectual tradition, but produced the very conceptual universe in which later thinkers and artists live and breathe. Even when they do not agree with particular formulations in Plato or Aristotle, they still perform, willingly or not, on the stage these thinkers built. Although, for example, one can trace the development of realism from Zeuxis to virtual reality, the basic idea that art can or should seek to reproduce the world is unthinkable without Plato. Zeuxis, Stendhal and Barthes represent different attitudes towards the same problem of representation. Mimesis is the inescapable conceptual medium of Western thinking about art, artists and audiences, and about their relationship to broader currents in human psychology and collective life.

With this notion in mind, I would like to conclude by discussing a recent and provocative development of the theory of mimesis that has had a broad impact in a number of sciences. In his influential 1976 book *The Selfish Gene*, the British zoologist Richard Dawkins proposes that human mental life may operate according to the same principles of evolution that determine physical life. Dawkins argues that theories of human culture based on biological advantage are largely unsatisfying because they explain culture only in terms of its usefulness for survival. In place of this account, he proposes the existence of a distinct unit of cultural evolution that operates independently of biological advantage. Physical life is governed by genes, tiny molecules that instruct the body to create specific proteins; intellectual and social life, Dawkins suggests, is governed by units of imitation he calls 'memes'. A meme, he writes, is 'an entity which is capable of being transmitted from one brain to another' (Dawkins, 1976: 210). Memes can be anything that survives through imitation, from ideas to songs to ritual practices. The idea passed from teacher to student, the song you hear on the car radio and continue humming at work, and the religious observances parents expect their children to respect are all examples of memes.

Although no one has discovered a material entity that might prove the existence of memes, a significant group of philosophers, psychologists and evolutionary biologists has taken up Dawkins' idea. The psychologist Susan Blackmore notes that genetic evolution is based on three major principles: variation, selection and heredity. Species emerge and develop because of genetic variations or mutations that prove valuable. Certain variations are favoured by natural and sexual selection (survival of the fittest and the choice of mates), and are passed down through the generations rather than vanishing with the organism that carries them. Blackmore offers the example of a well-known urban legend to illustrate these principles in memes as well. The story of the woman who tried to dry her unfortunate poodle in a microwave oven is familiar throughout Europe and America. It 'survives' as a recognizable narrative despite being told in different ways and incorporating new details (variation); it is chosen for retelling from among the thousands of stories that might also be told (selection); and it is recognizable to generations of school children despite variations in each particular telling (heredity) (Blackmore, 1999: 14–15). Seen in terms of genetic theory, the legend of the microwaved poodle is a set of instructions that, very much like the genes parents pass on to their children, creates a distinct but recognizable 'being' with each new repetition. The philosopher and cognitive theorist Daniel Dennett points to the example of Plato's influence. Although the original medium on which Plato wrote was probably lost not long after Plato himself died, Plato's ideas (the Platonic memes) have survived over time and in many different variations, and are now replicated in millions of books and carried about in hundreds of millions of minds (Dennett, 1991: 205–6).

Whereas genes survive by means of human sexual reproduction, then, memes survive through human imitation. Memes are by no means always beneficial to the organism, as anyone who has been kept awake at night by an all-too-catchy song can attest. The practice of celibacy among Catholic clergy, similarly, actively opposes the reproduction of the organism that imitates it (Dawkins, 1976: 213). Like genes, memes aim for little more than their own replication and imitation. But this does not mean that they are alien intruders or mere 'viruses of the mind', as some have termed them. Blackmore argues that memes are 'the very stuff of our minds' (1999: 22). For Dennett, the mind is 'a huge complex of memes' that functions somewhat like the software in a computer, which tells the hardware what procedures to perform (1991:

210). Installed by education and perception, the memes of culture collectively direct the operations of our brains. Biology is the hardware, culture the software. This analogy raises powerful questions about the nature of thought and consciousness. For writers such as Dennett, memes 'think' us, use our brains merely to replicate themselves as it were. 'A scholar', he writes, 'is just a library's way of making another library' (Dennett, 1991: 202). Although we tend to consider ourselves the abiding and autonomous spectator of the thoughts that pass through our brains, Dennett argues that consciousness is an illusion produced by the interaction of memes, and serves mostly for their advantage.

The theory of mimesis, we might suggest, is among the most successful memes in history. But even more than a single idea, mimesis is what memeologists would call a 'memeplex', a co-adapted group of ideas or practices that tend to be imitated together. Religions are especially good examples of memeplexes, since they involve many different objects of imitation – beliefs, rituals, architectural styles, music, written traditions – in a unified conceptual grouping. The memeplex of mimesis has had an equally complex legacy, shaping the works of intellectuals and artists alike since ancient Greece. Indeed, the idea of memes suggests that this memeplex has found yet another willing host. Although proponents of memetics find their inspiration in Darwinian theories of evolution, the meme is very much a part of the larger history of mimesis. Like role models, the imagery of theatre, the problem of realism, the theory of psychological identification or sympathetic magic, the notion that imitation is fundamental to human nature arose alongside the theory of mimesis in its Greek origins and seems to accompany the thematic complex whenever it is replicated.

Memetics seeks a biological origin and purpose in human intellectual and artistic creation. Like so many of the theories we have discussed in this book, it tries to explain cultural products and behaviours in bio-anthropological terms. The theory of memes, in this regard, is unthinkable without the philosophical concept of mimesis. Blackmore begins her book by perhaps unwittingly imitating one of the oldest memes of the theory of mimesis: that humans can best be distinguished from animals by their facility with imitation. 'We are so oblivious to the cleverness of imitation', she writes, 'that we do not even notice how rare it is in other animals, and how often we do it ourselves' (Blackmore,

1999: 4). Blackmore never cites Aristotle or Plato, but her 'oblivious' imitation of them suggests that the principles of mimesis have been so successful, have become so well established in the human 'meme pool', that they are part of the very genetic make-up of Western thought. The truths of nature and culture are so intertwined that it is now impossible to tell one from the other.

In fact, it might be argued that the theory of mimesis is both a symptom and cause of this confusion, rather than a useful way to sort it out. How can one ever know where nature ends and culture begins? The theory of mimesis ostensibly tries to solve this problem, but really only covers up a problem that is not open to solution. Mimesis, from this perspective, simply asks the wrong questions about the nature and origins of art. As I have suggested throughout this book, there is nothing inevitable or exclusive about the theory of mimesis. Many non-Western cultures have different ideas about art and imitation, and even within Western culture one finds a very wide range of attitudes towards the theory. Yet mimesis has so imposed itself on our thinking that it is often repeated as an unquestionable truth rather than regarded as a philosophical concept originating in Plato's dialogues, and passed down through numerous intellectual and artistic networks, and in a wide range of familiar themes and concepts. This is by no means to argue that we could simply dispense with mimesis, only that we need to recognize it as a theory with a history. There are many different ways into the thematic complex of mimesis, but for Western culture at least, there has been no way out of it.

GLOSSARY

Aesthetics Philosophical study of beauty in art and nature. Aestheticism was a movement in nineteenth-century art and literature that argued for the importance of beauty over moral teaching in art.

Antiquity General term referring to ancient Greek and Roman art, thought and society. Also referred to as classical antiquity.

Catharsis Greek word meaning 'purgation', which Aristotle used to describe the effects of tragedy on the audience (see chapter 2).

Convention An unspoken and normally traditional, but not necessarily unconscious, rule or agreement that guides social or artistic practice.

Epic Long narrative poem written in an elevated style that recounts the story of a hero, often drawn from myth. The form begins with Homer's *Iliad* and *Odyssey* (*c.*850 BCE), and became common in Western literature from Rome to the eighteenth century.

Identification Term used by Freud (see chapter 6) to describe the way unconscious imitations of others contribute to the formation of identity. Introjection describes the process by which identifications are psychologically internalized.

Ideology In common parlance, a set of political ideas or positions, but for Marx and subsequent thinkers, it describes our distorted or, in Althusser's terms, 'imaginary' relationship to the real conditions of existence, and in particular the way the interests of the ruling class come to seem natural and eternal.

Linear perspective A technical innovation in Renaissance painting that allowed for the illusion of three-dimensional space on a two-dimensional surface (see chapter 5).

Ode Ancient genre of lyric poetry that typically treats a noble or elevated subject in a meditative or ecstatic manner.

Oedipus complex Term used by Freud to describe a young boy's simultaneous love for his mother and rivalry with his father (see chapter 6).

Pastoral Formal poetic and prose genre focusing on the lives of rural characters, especially shepherds.

Performative Term drawn from linguistic philosophy describing the way certain utterances, such as promising, do not describe a state of affairs but make something happen. Gender theorists have adapted the term to account for the way gender identity is a kind of act rather than an essence. Performance studies is a recently developed academic field focusing on ideas of performance across cultures.

Postmodern As a period term, this generally refers to art and literature produced from the 1950s to the 1990s, and the social conditions that it epitomizes. As a formal term, it is distinguished from modernism, which refers to experimental works from roughly 1910 to 1940. Postmodernism in art is marked by parody, eclecticism and the incorporation of popular cultural forms.

Renaissance Meaning 'rebirth', a period in European art and thought, beginning in fourteenth-century Italy and ending in the seventeenth century, marked by a revival of interest in classical antiquity (see above).

Representation General term describing the way one thing (an image, a politician, a symbol) stands or speaks for another. Used in the context of critical theory, it is a near-synonym for mimesis, though often wider in application.

Romanticism European literary and artistic movement beginning in the late eighteenth century, valuing originality, imagination, emotion and the natural world.

Tragedy Dramatic genre beginning in ancient Greece that typically depicted the fall of a noble or mythic hero in a high and serious tone.

Vernacular A language native to a region or country, as opposed to a scholarly, literary, technical or foreign language. In Europe, the vernaculars, such as French or Italian, are thus differentiated from Latin.

Suggestions for Further Reading

SURVEYS, GENERAL DISCUSSIONS AND COLLECTIONS OF ESSAYS

Dautenhahn, Kerstin, and Chrystopher L. Nehaniv, eds (2002) *Imitation in Animals and Artifacts*, Cambridge MA: MIT Press.
Interdisciplinary collection of essays on imitation in animals, children and robots. Relatively technical, but still accessible.

Gebauer, Gunter, and Christoph Wulf [1992] (1995) *Mimesis: Culture, Art, Society*, trans. Don Reneau, Berkeley CA: University of California Press.
A detailed history of mimesis from Plato to Derrida that traces the changing relationship between aesthetic and social inflections of the theory.

Halliwell, Stephen (2002) *The Aesthetics of Mimesis: Ancient Texts, Modern Problems*, Princeton NJ: Princeton University Press.
Extensive discussion of mimesis in Plato and Aristotle that follows the influence of their ideas into present thinking about aesthetics.

Lacoue-Labarthe, Philippe (1998) *Typography: Mimesis, Philosophy, Politics*, trans. Christopher Fynsk and others, Stanford CA: Stanford University Press.
Influential series of philosophical essays on mimesis in the work of Plato, Hölderlin, Diderot, Girard, Heidegger and others.

IMITATIO AND ROMANTICISM

Abrams, M. H. (1971) *The Mirror and the Lamp*, New York and London: Oxford University Press.
Still the most comprehensive study of the relationship between Romantic theories of art and traditional ideas about mimesis and *imitatio*.

Bloom, Harold (1973) *The Anxiety of Influence*, New York and London: Oxford University Press.
Influential discussion of the way post-Romantic poets write out of a sense of belatedness in relation to their great predecessors.

Greene, Thomas M. (1982) *The Light in Troy: Imitation and Discovery in Renaissance Poetry*, New Haven CT: Yale University Press.
A classic study of Renaissance *imitatio*, with a discussion of ancient theories and illuminating readings of works by Petrarch, Erasmus and others.

THEATRE AND THEATRICALITY

Barish, Jonas (1981) *The Antitheatrical Prejudice*, Berkeley CA: University of California Press.
A wide-ranging study of antitheatrical attitudes from Plato to the twentieth century.

Diamond, Elin (1997) *Unmaking Mimesis*, London and New York: Routledge.
Influential essays on the intersection between traditional theories of mimesis and the practice of feminist theatre.

Fried, Michael (1980) *Absorption and Theatricality*, Chicago IL: University of Chicago Press.
An important account of the ways eighteenth-century painters reconfigured the relationship between painting and the beholder by turning against theatricality.

Schechner, Richard [1977] (2003) *Performance Theory*, London and New York: Routledge.
Intellectually challenging essays on cross-cultural ideas about theatre by one of the founders of performance studies.

REALISM

Auerbach, Erich [1946] (2003) *Mimesis*, trans. Willard Trask, Princeton NJ: Princeton University Press.
Classic study of Western realism from Homer and the Bible to Virginia Woolf.

Gombrich, E. H. (1960) *Art and Illusion*, Princeton NJ: Princeton University Press.
Somewhat dated but still illuminating study of artistic realism that draws on scientific accounts of perception and cognition to explain how we recognize the real in art.

Nochlin, Linda (1971) *Realism*, London: Penguin.
Accessible discussion of pictorial realism and the realist movement in nineteenth-century painting.

Prendergast, Christopher (1986) *The Order of Mimesis*, Cambridge: Cambridge University Press.
Incisive critical discussion of mimesis, along with readings of works by nineteenth-century realist writers such as Balzac and Stendhal.

IDENTIFICATION

Borch-Jacobsen, Mikkel [1982] (1988) *The Freudian Subject*, trans. Catherine Porter, Stanford CA: Stanford University Press.
Dense and difficult, but influential, discussion of Freud's theory of identification.

Butler, Judith [1990] (1999) *Gender Trouble: Feminism and the Subversion of Identity*, New York and London: Routledge.
Challenging and important account of gender as a 'compulsory performance'.

Fuss, Diana (1995) *Identification Papers*, New York and London: Routledge.
A witty, perceptive and mostly accessible discussion of identification in the work of Freud, Fanon and others.

MIMESIS AND CULTURE

Baudrillard, Jean [1981] (1994) *Simulacra and Simulations*, trans. Sheila Faria Glaser, Ann Arbor: University of Michigan Press.
Includes the influential essay, 'The Precession of Simulacra', along with shorter reflections on holograms, cloning and other examples of the hyperreal.

Girard, René [1972] (1977) *Violence and the Sacred*, trans. Patrick Gregory, Baltimore MD: The Johns Hopkins University Press.
Dense and wide-ranging study of mimetic desire and sacrifice in mythology, ritual, Greek tragedy and Freudian psychoanalysis.

Schwartz, Hillel (1996) *The Culture of the Copy*, New York: Zone Books.
Gathers a dizzying array of copies and likenesses, with an emphasis on examples of doubling and duplication in modern culture.

Taussig, Michael (1993) *Mimesis and Alterity*, New York and London: Routledge.
Wide-ranging account of the 'mimetic faculty' as it arises in instances of contact between modern colonial and indigenous cultures.

BIBLIOGRAPHY

Alberti, L. B. (1991) *On Painting*, trans. C. Grayson, London: Penguin.

Althusser, L. (1971) *Lenin and Philosophy*, trans. B. Brewster, New York: Monthly Review Press.

Aristotle (1951) *Aristotle's Theory of Poetry and Fine Art*, trans. S. H. Butcher, New York: Dover.

Artaud, A. (1958) *The Theater and Its Double*, trans. M. C. Richards, New York: Grove Press.

Auerbach, E. (1974) *Mimesis: The Representation of Reality in Western Literature*, trans. W. Trask, Princeton NJ: Princeton University Press.

Augustine (1961) *Confessions*, trans. R. S. Pine-Coffin, Harmondsworth: Penguin.

Barish, J. (1981) *The Antitheatrical Prejudice*, Berkeley CA: University of California Press.

Barthes, R. (1974) *S/Z*, trans. R. Miller, New York: Farrar Straus and Giroux.

—— (1986) *The Rustle of Language*, trans. R. Howard, Berkeley CA: University of California Press.

Baudelaire, C. (1965) *Art in Paris, 1845–1862: Reviews of Salons and Other Exhibitions*, trans. J. Mayne, London: Phaidon.

Baudrillard, J. (1994) *Simulacra and Simulations*, trans. S. F. Glaser, Ann Arbor: University of Michigan Press.

Becker, G. J. (ed.) (1963) *Documents of Modern Literary Realism*, Princeton NJ: Princeton University Press.

Benjamin, W. (1978) 'On the Mimetic Faculty', trans. E. Jephcott, in P. Demetz (ed.) *Reflections*, New York: Schocken.

Bhabha, H. (1994) *The Location of Culture*, London: Routledge.

Blackmore, S. (1999) *The Meme Machine*, Oxford: Oxford University Press.

Bloom, H. (1973) *The Anxiety of Influence*, London: Oxford University Press.

Blumenberg, H. (1977) 'The Concept of Reality and the Possibility of the Novel', in R. E. Amacher and V. Lange (eds) *New Perspectives in German Literary Criticism*, Princeton NJ: Princeton University Press.

Borch-Jacobsen, M. (1988) *The Freudian Subject*, trans. C. Porter, Stanford CA: Stanford University Press.

Borges, J. L. (1998) *Collected Fictions*, trans. A. Hurley, New York: Viking.

Brecht, B. (1964) *Brecht on Theater*, trans. J. Willett, New York: Hill and Wang.

Butler, J. (1991) 'Imitation and Gender Insubordination', in D. Fuss (ed.) *Inside/Out: Lesbian Theories, Gay Theories*, New York: Routledge.

Caillois, R. (1961) *Man, Play, and Games*, trans. M. Barish, New York: Free Press.

—— (1984) 'Mimicry and Legendary Psychasthenia', trans. J. Shepley, *October*, 31, 16–32.

Cassirer, E., Kristeller, P. O. and Randall Jr, J. H. (eds) (1948) *The Renaissance Philosophy of Man*, Chicago IL: University of Chicago Press.
Christian, L. G. (1987) *Theatrum Mundi: The History of an Idea*, New York: Garland.
Dante (1982) *Inferno*, trans. A. Mandelbaum, New York: Bantam.
Dawkins, R. (1976) *The Selfish Gene*, New York: Oxford University Press.
de Beauvoir, S. (1973) *The Second Sex*, trans. E. M. Parshley, New York: Vintage.
Debord, G. (1994) *Society of the Spectacle*, trans. D. Nicholson-Smith, New York: Zone.
Deleuze, G. (1990) *The Logic of Sense*, trans. M. Lester and C. Stivale, New York: Columbia University Press.
Dennett, D. (1991) *Consciousness Explained*, Boston MA: Little, Brown.
Derrida, J. (1981) *Dissemination*, trans. B. Johnson, Chicago IL: University of Chicago Press.
Descartes, R. (1998) *Discourse on Method and Meditations on First Philosophy*, trans. D. A. Cress, Indianapolis IN: Hackett.
Diamond, E. (1997) *Unmaking Mimesis: Essays on Feminism and Theater*, London: Routledge.
Diderot, D. (1994) *Selected Writings on Art and Literature*, trans. G. Bremner, Harmondsworth: Penguin.
Du Bellay, J. (2001) *La Deffence, et illustration de la langue françoyse*, Geneva: Droz.
Eliot, G. (1996) *Adam Bede*, Oxford: Oxford University Press.
Else, G. (1958) '"Imitation" in the Fifth Century', *Classical Philology*, 53, 73–90.
Evreinoff, N. (1970) *The Theater in Life*, trans. A. I. Nazaroff, New York: Benjamin Blom.
Fanon, F. (1967) *Black Skin, White Masks*, trans. C. L. Markmann, New York: Grove Press.
Fenichel, O. (1954) 'Identification', in *The Collected Papers of Otto Fenichel, First Series*, New York: Norton.
Féral, J. (2002) 'Theatricality: The Specificity of Theatrical Language', *SubStance*, 31, 94–108.
Frazer, J. (1922) *The Golden Bough*, New York: Macmillan.
Freud, S. (1953–74) *The Standard Edition of the Complete Psychological Works of Sigmund Freud*, trans. J. Strachey, London: Hogarth Press.
Fried, M. (1980) *Absorption and Theatricality*, Chicago IL: University of Chicago Press.
Fuss, D. (1995) *Identification Papers*, New York: Routledge.
Gebauer, G. and Wulf, C. (1995) *Mimesis: Culture, Art, Society*, trans. D. Reneau, Berkeley CA: University of California Press.
Girard, R. (1965) *Deceit, Desire, and the Novel*, trans. Y. Freccero, Baltimore MD: The Johns Hopkins University Press.
—— (1977) *Violence and the Sacred*, trans. P. Gregory, Baltimore MD: The Johns Hopkins University Press.
—— (1978) *To Double Business Bound: Essays on Literature, Mimesis, and Anthropology*, Baltimore MD: The Johns Hopkins University Press.

—— (1979) 'Mimesis and Violence: Perspectives in Cultural Criticism', *Berkshire Review*, 14, 9–19.

—— (1987) *Things Hidden Since the Foundation of the World*, trans. S. Bann and M. Metteer, Stanford CA: Stanford University Press.

—— (1991) *A Theater of Envy: William Shakespeare*, New York: Oxford University Press.

Goffman, E. (1959) *The Presentation of Self in Everyday Life*, New York: Anchor.

Golden, L. (1992) *Aristotle on Tragic and Comic Mimesis*, Atlanta GA: Scholars Press.

Goodman, N. (1968) *Languages of Art*, Indianapolis IN: Bobbs-Merrill.

Gran, A.-B. (2002) 'The Fall of Theatricality in the Age of Modernity', *SubStance*, 31, 251–64.

Greenblatt, S. (1980) *Renaissance Self-fashioning from More to Shakespeare*, Chicago IL: University of Chicago Press.

Greene, T. M. (1982) *The Light in Troy: Imitation and Discovery in Renaissance Poetry*, New Haven: Yale University Press.

Grube, G. M. A. (1965) *The Greek and Roman Critics*, London: Methuen.

Halliwell, S. (2002) *The Aesthetics of Mimesis*, Princeton NJ: Princeton University Press.

Havelock, E. A. (1963) *Preface to Plato*, Cambridge MA: Harvard University Press.

Hayne, H., Herbert, J. and Simcock, G. (2003) 'Imitation from Television by 24- and 30-month-olds', *Developmental Science*, 6, 254–61.

Heidegger, M. (1998) *Pathmarks*, ed. W. McNeill, Cambridge: Cambridge University Press.

Horace (1999) *The Complete Odes and Satires of Horace*, trans. S. Alexander, Princeton, NJ: Princeton University Press.

Horkheimer, M. and Adorno, T. W. (1972) *Dialectic of Enlightenment*, trans. J. Cumming, New York: Continuum.

Irigaray, L. (1985) *This Sex Which Is Not One*, trans. C. Porter, Ithaca NY: Cornell University Press.

Jakobson, R. (1987) *Language in Literature*, eds K. Pomorska and S. Rudy, Cambridge MA: Harvard University Press.

James, H. (1984) 'The Art of Fiction', in L. Edel (ed.) *Literary Criticism*, Vol. 1, New York: Library of America.

Kant, I. (1987) *Critque of Judgment*, trans. W. S. Pluhar, Indianapolis IN: Hackett.

Kofman, S. (1999) *Camera Obscura: Of Ideology*, trans. W. Straw, Ithaca NY: Cornell University Press.

Kohansky, M. (1984) *The Disreputable Profession*, Westport CT: Greenwood Press.

Lacan, J. (1977) *Écrits: A Selection*, trans. A. Sheridan, New York: Norton.

Lacoue-Labarthe, P. (1998) *Typography: Mimesis, Philosophy, Politics*, trans. C. Fynsk and others, Stanford CA: Stanford University Press.

Laplanche, J. (1976) *Life and Death in Psychoanalysis*, trans. J. Mehlman, Baltimore MD: The Johns Hopkins University Press.

Lessing, G. E. (1962) *Hamburg Dramaturgy*, trans. V. Lange, New York: Dover.

Lukács, G. (2002) *Studies in European Realism*, trans. E. Bone, New York: Howard Fertig.
Machiavelli, N. (1995) *The Prince and Other Political Writings*, trans. S. Milner, London: J. M. Dent.
Mallarmé, S. (1982) *Selected Poetry and Prose*, ed. M. A. Caws, New York: New Directions.
Marshall, D. (1986) *The Figure of Theater*, New York: Columbia University Press.
Marx, K. (1978) *The Marx-Engels Reader*, ed. R. C. Tucker, New York: Norton.
Mauss, M. (1972) *A General Theory of Magic*, trans. R. Brain, London: Routledge and Kegan Paul.
Metz, C. (1974) *Film Language: A Semiotics of the Cinema*, trans. M. Taylor, New York: Oxford University Press.
Mukarovsky, J. (1978) *Structure, Sign, and Function*, eds J. Burbank and P. Steiner, New Haven: Yale University Press.
Nochlin, L. (1971) *Realism*, London: Penguin.
Orgel, S. (1981) 'The Renaissance Artist as Plagiarist', *ELH*, 48, 476–95.
Ovid (1955) *Metamorphoses*, trans. R. Humphries, Bloomington IN: Indiana University Press.
Panofsky, E. (1997) *Perspective as Symbolic Form*, trans. C. S. Wood, New York: Zone.
Plato (1989) *The Collected Dialogues*, eds E. Hamilton and H. Cairns, Princeton NJ: Princeton University Press.
—— (1991) *Republic*, trans. A. Bloom, New York: Basic Books.
Pliny (1952) *Natural History*, trans. H. Rackham, London: Heinemann.
Pope, A. (1971) 'An Essay on Criticism', in H. Adams (ed.) *Critical Theory Since Plato*, San Diego: Harcourt Brace Jovanovich.
Reynolds, J. (1997) *Discourses on Art*, New Haven and London: Yale University Press.
Riviere, J. (1991) *Collected Papers: 1920–1958*, London: Karnac Books.
Rousseau, J.-J. (1960) *Politics and the Arts: Letter to M. d'Alembert on the Theater*, trans. A. Bloom, Ithaca NY: Cornell University Press.
—— (1979) *Emile, or On Education*, trans. A. Bloom, New York: Basic Books.
Russell, D. A. and Winterbottom, M. (eds) (1972) *Ancient Literary Criticism: The Principal Texts in New Translations*, Oxford: Oxford University Press.
Schechner, R. (2003) *Performance Theory*, London: Routledge.
Seneca (1920) *Epistles 66–92*, trans, R. Gummere, Cambridge MA: Harvard University Press.
Shakespeare, W. (1974) *The Riverside Shakespeare*, Boston: Houghton Mifflin.
Sidney, P. (2002) *An Apology for Poetry*, Manchester: Manchester University Press.
Stendhal (1953) *Scarlet and Black*, trans. M. Shaw, Harmondsworth: Penguin.
Tarde, G. (1962) *The Laws of Imitation*, trans. E. C. Parsons, Gloucester MA: Peter Smith.
Tatarkiewicz, W. (1973–4) 'Mimesis', in P. P. Wiener (ed.) *Dictionary of the History of Ideas*, New York: Scribner's.
Taussig, M. (1993) *Mimesis and Alterity*, New York: Routledge.

Trachtenberg, A. (ed.) (1980) *Classic Essays on Photography*, New Haven: Leete's Island Books.

Turner, V. (1982) *From Ritual to Theater*, New York: PAJ Publications.

Vernant, J.-P. (1991) *Mortals and Immortals*, ed. F. I. Zeitlin, Princeton NJ: Princeton University Press.

Weber, S. (2004) *Theatricality as Medium*, New York: Fordham University Press.

Weimann, R. (1985) 'Mimesis in *Hamlet*', in P. Parker and G. Hartman (eds) *Shakespeare and the Question of Theory*, London: Methuen.

Wellek, R. (1963) 'The Concept of Realism in Literary Scholarship', in S. G. Nichols (ed.) *Concepts of Criticism*, New Haven and London: Yale University Press.

Wilde, O. (1982) *The Artist as Critic*, Chicago: University of Chicago Press.

Williams, R. (1983) *Keywords*, New York: Oxford University Press.

Winckelmann, J. J. (1987) *Reflections on the Imitation of Greek Works in Painting and Sculpture*, trans. E. Heyer and R. C. Norton, La Salle IL: Open Court.

Young, E. (1971) 'Conjectures on Original Composition', in H. Adams (ed.) *Critical Theory Since Plato*, San Diego: Harcourt Brace Jovanovich.

Index

actors and acting 5, 8, 16, 18, 20, 28, 29, 49, 72, 73, 77, 116, 119–20, 130, 131, 136, 152; in eighteenth-century thought 82–5; in Shakespeare 76, 78–82; and social conventions 74–6; in twentieth-century thought 85–91; *see also* theatricality
Adorno, Theodor 10, 140, 146, 153; *Dialectic of Enlightenment, The* 144–5
Alberti, Leon Battista: *On Painting* 100–1
Althusser, Louis: 'Ideology and Ideological State Apparatuses' 128
Aristotle 2, 3, 4, 5, 6, 7, 9, 16, 32–46, 49, 50, 63, 64, 65, 73, 75, 88, 90, 97, 98, 103, 105, 106, 107, 111, 115, 123, 136, 149, 157, 158, 161; *Poetics* 7, 16, 32–46, 90; on reason 38–45; on tragic emotions 43–6; on tragic plot 39–42
Artaud, Antonin 46; *Theater and Its Double* 85
Auerbach, Erich 9, 109, 157; *Mimesis* 104, 105–7
Augustine 8, 73, 87, 157; *Confessions* 63, 71–2
Austen, Jane: *Mansfield Park* 83

Balzac, Honoré de 95, 104, 105, 107, 109, 111
Barish, Jonas 72
Barthes, Roland 9, 158; 'Reality Effect, The' 99; *S/Z* 109–11
Battle of Ancients and Moderns 65–6
Baudelaire, Charles: *Salon* of 1859 108, 109
Baudrillard, Jean: *Simulacra and Simulations* 154–6
Beauvoir, Simone de 128
Benjamin, Walter 10, 143, 144, 145, 153; 'Mimetic Faculty, The' 140–2
Bhabha, Homi: 'Of Mimicry and Man' 133–4
Blackmore, Susan 159, 160–1
Blake, William 68–9, 70
Bloom, Harold 69
Blumenberg, Hans 93
Borch-Jacobsen, Mikkel 119–20, 125
Borges, Jorge Luis 11
Brecht, Bertolt 8, 85–6, 87, 109, 119, 130, 157; *Mother Courage* 86
Butler, Judith 129, 134, 157; 'Imitation and Gender Insubordination' 131–2

Caillois, Roger 10, 140, 144, 145, 153; *Man, Play, and Games* 143; 'Mimicry and Legendary Psychasthenia' 142–3
catharsis 45–6, 80, 85, 119, 149
Cervantes, Miguel de 147; *Don Quixote* 60–1
children, childhood 2, 3, 18–19, 21, 26, 27, 28, 30, 36–7, 38, 53, 57–8, 88, 115, 116, 120, 123–8, 132–3, 135, 141, 146
Christian, Lynda G. 76
conventions, social and artistic 4–5, 9, 50–1, 52, 53, 54, 67, 68, 74–5, 84, 86, 87, 88, 97–102, 105, 109–11, 129, 130, 132
copyright 69–70

Dante Aligheri 64, 95; *Inferno* 53, 61
Darwin, Charles 117, 160
Dawkins, Richard: *Selfish Gene, The* 158, 159
Debord, Guy: *Society of the Spectacle, The* 153–4
Deleuze, Gilles 150, 153, 154; 'Plato and the Simulacrum' 151–2
Dennett, Daniel 159, 160
Derrida, Jacques 2, 150, 154; 'Double Session, The' 152–3
Descartes, René: *Discourse on Method* 65–6
Desnoyers, Fernand 98
Diamond, Elin 130
Diderot, Denis 8, 86, 116, 119, 157; 'Parodox of the Actor, The' 83–5
Dionysius of Halicarnassus 56
Dreiser, Theodore 102
Du Bellay, Joachim: *Defence and Illustration of the French Language* 60

Eliot, George 108, 109, 157; *Adam Bede* 103–4
Erasmus 8, 54, 69
Evreinoff, Nicolas: *Theater in Life, The* 87–9

Fanon, Franz: *Black Skin, White Masks* 132–3, 134
Fenichel, Otto 122
Féral, Josette 8, 74, 76
Flaubert, Gustave 105, 107
Frazer, James 140, 144, 156; *Golden Bough, The* 138–9
Freud, Sigmund 9, 46, 116, 125, 128, 132, 134, 135, 136, 137, 140, 143, 144, 157; on identification 118–24; *Interpretation of Dreams, The* 121
Fried, Michael 82
Fuss, Diana 122, 133, 134

Gebauer, Gunter 6, 82, 157
Girard, René 10, 145–50; *Deceit, Desire, and The Novel* 146–8, 149; *Theater of Envy, A* 150
Goethe, Johann Wolfgang: *Sorrows of Young Werther* 3; *Wilhelm Meister's Apprenticeship* 82
Goffman, Erving 8, 131; *Presentation of Self in Everyday Life, The* 89–90
Goodman, Nelson 101–2, 109; *Languages of Art* 95
Gran, Anne-Britt 75
Greenblatt, Stephen 77
Greene, Thomas 53, 61
Grube, G. M. A. 54

Halliwell, Stephen 3, 37
Havelock, Eric 30
Heidegger, Martin 22
Homer 26, 27, 30, 41, 51, 52, 53, 67, 106; *Iliad* 24, 41, 52; *Odyssey*, 24, 42, 105
Horace 7, 52, 55–6, 57, 59
Horkheimer, Max: *Dialectic of Enlightenment, The* 144–5; *see also* Adorno, Theodor
Hubert, Henri: *General Theory of Magic, A* 139

identification 1, 9, 43–4, 84, 85, 115, 129–30, 132–5, 136, 139, 144, 160; for Freud 118–25; for Lacan 125–28 *see also* Freud, Sigmund
ideology 10, 137, 157; *see also* Marx, Karl
imitatio 7, 8, 49–70; in ancient Rome 54–9; decline of 65–70; and emulation 56–7; and parody 53; in Renaissance 59–65
Irigaray, Luce 130, 131, 134

Jakobson, Roman 99; 'On Realism in Art' 96
James, Henry 94
Joyce, James 53

Kant, Immanuel: *Critique of Judgement* 67, 68
Kofman, Sarah 138
Kohansky, Mendel 72

Lacan, Jacques 9, 140, 143; 'Mirror Stage as Formative of the Function of the "I", The' 125–8
Lacoue-Labarthe, Philippe 19, 135; 'Typography' 116
Laplanche, Jean 120
Lessing, G. E.: *Hamburg Dramaturgy* 45–6
Longinus 7; On the Sublime' 58–9
Lukács, Georg 9, 103, 107, 109; *Studies in European Realism* 104–5

Machiavelli, Niccolò: *Prince, The* 77–8
magic 9–10, 138–45, 153, 155, 156, 160
Mallarmé, Stéphane 152–3
Marshall, David 82
Marx, Karl 9, 117, 128, 140; *German Ideology, The* 137–8
Mauss, Marcel: *General Theory of Magic, A* 139
memes, memetics 10, 158–61
Metz, Christian 96
Milton, John: *Paradise Lost* 53
mimetic desire 145–50; *see also* Girard, René
mimicry 1, 2, 16, 27, 87, 131, 133–4, 140, 142–5
mirror stage 125–8, 143; *see also* Lacan, Jacques
Monet, Claude 96
Mukarovsky, Jan 74

Nochlin, Linda 98, 99

Oedipus complex 123–4, 129–30; *see also* Freud, Sigmund
Orgel, Stephen 62
Ovid 52; *Metamorphoses* 107–8

Panofsky, Erwin: 'Perspective as Symbolic Form' 100–1
perspective 8, 93, 96, 97, 100–2
Petrarch 8, 62–3, 157
Pico della Mirandola 78, 82; *Oration on the Dignity of Man* 77
Pierre de Blois 59, 62
Pindar 52, 55–6, 57
Plato 3, 5, 6, 7, 9, 15–31, 32, 33, 34, 36, 37, 38, 43, 45, 49, 50, 63, 64, 72, 73, 75, 77, 80, 92, 93, 94, 95, 97, 98, 102, 103, 106, 107, 109, 110, 111, 115, 116, 128, 135, 136, 138, 139, 140, 145, 149, 150, 151, 153, 154, 155, 157, 158, 159, 161; allegory of the cave 22, 29, 138; on education 18–21; on reason and emotion 26–7; *Republic* 2, 15, 17–31, 32, 33, 35, 38, 116; *Sophist* 151; on stories and storytelling 19–21; on tragedy 25–7
Pliny 95, 99–100; *Natural History* 92–3
Poe, Edgar Allen 96–7
Pope, Alexander 7, 66, 67, 68, 69; 'Essay on Criticism, an' 50–2
Proust, Marcel 147, 149
Pygmalion 107–8

Quintillian: *Institutio Oratoria* 56–7

realism 1, 5, 6, 8, 41, 49, 92–111, 158, 160; and anti-realism 9, 107–11; of film and photography 93, 96–7, 98–9, 108; in literature

94, 98, 99, 102–7, 109–11; magical 96; in painting 92–3, 96, 98, 100–2, 129
Reynolds, Joshua: *Discourses on Art* 68–9
Riviere, Joan: 'Womanliness as Masquerade' 129–30
role models, imitation of 6, 7, 8, 49, 50–2, 53, 58, 59, 60, 65, 68, 119, 120, 122, 124–5, 146, 160; *see also imitatio*
Rousseau, Jean-Jacques 8, 9, 85, 89, 138; *Emile* 136–7; *Letter to D'Alembert on the Theater* 83

Schechner, Richard 8, 74
Seneca 7, 52, 57–8, 59, 60
Shakespeare, William 8, 90, 149, 150, 157; *As You Like It* 76; *Hamlet* 8, 78–83, 150
Sidney, Philip 8; *Apology for Poetry* 64–5
simulacrum 10, 150–6
Socrates 15, 17–30, 33, 35, 36, 139; *see also* Plato
Sophocles 52; *Oedipus the King* 42, 123
Stendhal 104, 107, 108, 109, 147, 149, 158; *Scarlet and Black* 102–3

Tarde, Gabriel 9; *Laws of Imitation, The* 117–18
Taussig, Michael 139–40
theatricality 1, 6, 8, 18, 72, 78, 79, 80, 87–9, 121
theatrum mundi 8, 75–8, 81, 87
Tolstoy, Leo 99, 104, 105
tragedy 25–7, 29, 32, 33, 34, 35, 38–46, 72, 73, 75, 76, 90, 106
Turner, Victor 90–1

verisimilitude 1, 97
Vernant, Jean-Pierre 16–17,
Virgil 7, 51, 60, 69; *Aeneid* 52, 61, 63

Warhol, Andy 151–2
Weber, Samuel 73
Weimann, Robert 78
Wellek, René 95
Werther Effect 3
Wilde, Oscar 9, 111; 'Decay of Lying, The' 108–9
Williams, Raymond 94
Winckelmann, Johann Joachim: *Thoughts on the Imitation of Greek Works in Painting and Sculpture* 66
Wulf, Christoph 6, 82, 157

Young, Edward 69; *Conjectures on Original Composition* 66–7

Zola, Emile 98, 105